OLD SIDMOUTH

Compiled by

REGINALD LANE

Member of
Sidmouth Museum Committee

DEVON BOOKS

First published in 1990 by Devon Books
Reprinted in paperback in 1995 in association with
the Sid Vale Association (Sidmouth Museum).

British Library Cataloguing in Publication Data
Catalogue data for this book is available
from the British Library.

ISBN 086114 895 9

*The cover illustrations are taken from the journals
of Peter Orlando Hutchinson, reproduced here by
courtesy of the Devon Record Office and West Country
Studies Library. The front cover shows Peak Hill from
Sidmouth sketched on 16 June 1849. The back cover shows
Amyat Place and the Church Tower viewed from Coburg Terrace
and dated 29 July 1848.*

DEVON BOOKS
Official Publisher to Devon County Council
Halsgrove House
Lower Moor Way
Tiverton
Devon EX16 6SS
Tel: 01884 243242
Fax: 01884 243325

Printed and bound in Great Britain by The Devonshire Press Ltd, Torquay, Devon

CONTENTS

LIST OF SUBSCRIBERS

A

E.G. Andrews, *12 Trumps Court, Sidmouth*
J. Ankins, *43 Tyrrell Mead, Sidmouth*

B

D.J. and M. Baldock, *11a Newlands Close, Sidmouth*
Wendy Bartlett, *93 Higher Woolbrook Park, Sidmouth*
Mr and Mrs D.M. Basey, *Pinelands, Sid Road, Sidmouth*
Dennis R.J. Bennett, *Lilac Cottage, Greenhead, Sidbury*
Mr E. Bennett, *4 Woolbrook Rise, Sidmouth*
Mr and Mrs R.H. Bewshea, *2 Salcombe Court, Salcombe Hill Road, Sidmouth*
John and Pauline Bishop, *13 Burnards Close, Colyton*
Mrs K. Boutland, *Sunways, 33 Manstone Lane, Sidmouth*
Mr A.M. Bridgeman, *Fairway, Cottington Mead, Sidmouth*
Mrs P. Bromhead, *Beach House, The Esplanade, Sidmouth*

C

Mr and Mrs C. Carr, *Barrington Villa, Salcombe Road, Sidmouth*
Margaret Carter, *Oakdene, Higher Brook Meadow, Sidford, Sidmouth*
Margaret Clark, *4 Alexandria Road, Sidmouth*
Mr and Mrs C. Clapp, *Rosemount, Cottington Mead, Sidmouth*
Mrs Hazel Clapp, *42 Fleming Avenue, Sidmouth*
Mr Stanley Cooke, *Moorstones, 33 Summerfields, Sidmouth*
Miss Hermione Copleston, *1 Elwyn Court, Cranford Avenue, Exmouth*
G.M. Counter, *50 York Street, Sidmouth*
Mr and Mrs A.J. Cox, *10 Balfour Manor, Broadway, Sidmouth*
Julia Creeke, *Connaught House, Peak Hill Road, Sidmouth*

D

J.S.N. Dale, *Rydings, Cotlands, Cotmaton Road, Sidmouth*
Andrea and Robin Danielli, *The Kneelings, Dog Lane, Witcombe, Gloucester*
Mrs S. Davies, *Broadlea, 4 Manstone Mead, Sidmouth*
Aline and Michael Davis, *18 Roselands, Sidmouth*
Miss K.S. Dougill, *Newlands, 5 Sidgard Road, Sidmouth*
Chris and Carol Dunford, *Bergwen, Fortescue Road, Sidmouth*
Maurice and Ann Dunford, *Livonia House, Sidford Road, Sidmouth*
William E. Dunn, *Berwyn, Barnhayes, Sidmouth*
Philip A. Dwerryhouse, *Lime Parc, Bickwell Valley, Sidmouth*

E

M.A. Edgington, *22 Green Lane, Bournemouth*
Amy Catherine Eggar, *4 Saxon Croft, Farnham, Surrey*
Mr A.R. Enticott, *38 Woolbrook Park, Sidmouth*

F

R.S. Fearnehough, *Flat 1, Moorcourt, Moorcourt Close, Cotmaton Road, Sidmouth*
Mr and Mrs K.R. Felce, *8 College Street, Higham Ferrers, Northants*
Fields of Sidmouth, *Market Place, Sidmouth*
Dr and Mrs Hugh Forshaw, *Beverley, 25 Silverton Road, Aigburth, Liverpool*
Sara Fowler, *39 Foxcote, Wokingham, Berkshire*

G

E.J. Gauthier Graham, *Montrose, Elverway Cottages, Branscombe*
R.W. Gillam, *Cranleigh, 65 Peaslands Road, Sidmouth*
Margaret and Derek Gobbett, *Birchley Hall Cottage, Windmill Lane, Corley*
Mr and Mrs R. Goodenough, *25 Ernsborough Gardens, Honiton*
Miriam Greaves, *The Reef, Boughmore Road, Sidmouth*
C.W. Green (President, Sid Vale Association), *Old Barn Cottage, Salcombe Regis, Sidmouth*
Mr and Mrs T. Greene, *Bridge House, Mill Street, Sidmouth*
Rev B.W. Greenup, *Barton Cottage, Coburg Road, Sidmouth*
Mr B.C.V. Greer, *The Shrubbery, Vicarage Road, Sidmouth*
Mr and Mrs J.A. Griffin, *Burgh House, Knowle Drive, Sidmouth*

H

Miss M.J. Hall, *14 Powys House, All Saints Road, Sidmouth*
Mr and Mrs H.T. Hancock, *38 Malden Road, Sidmouth*
Mrs Peggy Harbud, *Bramley Dene, Connaught Close, Sidmouth*
James C. Hartas, *18 Fleming Avenue, Sidford*
B.W. Hartley, *Culverden, Bickwell Lane, Sidmouth*
Mike and Maureen Hartnell, *36 Newtown, Sidmouth*
Mr and Mrs R.W. Haward, *Core Edge, Windsor Mead, Sidford*
Daphne and Frank Hawkins, *The Stable, Bowd Court, Sidmouth*
Mrs I.J. Hebert, *Minstead, 63 Alexandria Road, Sidmouth*
Mr David M. Hines, *The Rocket House, Alma Lane, Sidmouth*
Miss C. Hodder, *1 Knowle Grange, Knowle Drive, Sidmouth*
Mrs M.E. Hodnett, *2 Fortfield Gardens, Sidmouth*
Miss K. Holroyde, *16 Connaught Road, Sidmouth*
Peter and Rosemary Hook, *Royal York and Faulkner Hotel, Esplanade, Sidmouth*
Joyce and Derek House, *25 Hamhaugh Island, Shepperton, Middlesex*
Alan and Eileen M. Hunt, *7 Meadowview Close, Sidmouth*

J

Mrs Trina Jarrett, *Hillhead St Mary, Broadway, Sidmouth*
C. and M. Jeary, *Daisy Bank, Convent Road, Sidmouth*
Harry John, *4 Path Whorlands, Sidmouth*
Mrs Anne Jones, *4 Stillions Close, Windmill Hill, Alton, Hants.*

K

Irene Keep, *Robins Croft, 9 Davids Close, Sidbury*
Mrs E.H. Kidman Cox
Miss Jill Kidman Cox
Mr and Mrs Kinder, *23 Pitchcombe Gardens, Coombe Dingle, Bristol*
Mr and Mrs Austin Knight, *8 Woolbrook Meadows, Sidmouth*
William A.C. Knight, *132 Malden Road, Sidmouth*
Bernard Korda, *Mayside, Blackmore View, Sidmouth*
Julia Kumik, *7 Glasshouse Lane, Exeter*

L

Doreen and Victor Lawrence, *372 London Road, St Albans, Herts*
Mrs Sheila Alice Lewis, *109 Woolbrook Road, Sidmouth*
Anthony Lister, *Deane Court, Westwell, Ashford, Kent*
Mrs J.O. Lobb, *43 Newlands Road, Sidmouth*
Robert and Priscilla Lobley, *Pebblestone Cottage, Sidmouth*
Cllr F.H.J. Lock, *31 High Meadow, Sidmouth*
Mr A.F.H. Love, *Redwalls, 31 Benfleet Close, Sutton, Surrey*

Miss Joan Luxton, *1 Cherryhayes Cottages, High Street, Sidmouth*
Sheila Luxton, *201 Manstone Avenue, Sidmouth*

M

W.B. and J.E. Macfarlane, *14 Primley Road, Sidmouth*
Derek J. Manley, *Courtlands, 2 Kingsley Avenue, Southbourne, Bournemouth*
Mr H. Marchant, *90 Peaslands Road, Sidmouth*
Miss J.W. Marr, *Styal, Kestell Road, Sidmouth*
Mrs E. Marsh, *10 Powys House, Sidmouth*
David Matthews, *3 Glebe Way, Wisborough Green, Billingshurst, West Sussex*
R.W. Meadows, *1 Green Mount, Sidmouth*
W.D. Mills, *2 Malden Road, Sidmouth*
B. Minton, *Danetree, Coreway, Sidford*
Gwen Mitchell, *Christchurch, New Zealand*
Maureen and John Mitchell, *Briarleigh, Yardelands Close, Sidmouth*
Mr and Mrs D. Moutarde, *Nancherrow, 92 Woolbrook Road, Sidmouth*
Mrs Betty Moxon, *Roselands, Latchmoor, Thorverton*

N

Leslie Harold Newall, *12 Lusways Court, Salcombe Hill Road, Sidmouth*
Mr and Mrs J. Newton, *Cedar Mead, Knowle Drive, Sidmouth*
The Ven. E.M. Norfolk, *5 Fairlawn Court, Sidmouth*
Sarah Northcott, *Palmdene, Burnt Oak, Sidbury*
Mr S.C. Nutt, *2 Fairleigh, Manor Road, Sidmouth*

O

David Oldfield, *39 Woodside Road, Beaumont Park, Huddersfield*
Mrs N. Osbourne-Moss, *Lindum, Knowle Drive, Sidmouth*
Mr and Mrs J.J. Osmond, *85 Higher Woolbrook Park, Sidmouth*

P

Elizabeth Palmer, *Waterview, 8 Barrington Mead, Sidmouth*
M.E. Passmore, *Market Post Office, Sidmouth*
Joan and Noel Paulson, *28 Cottington Court, Sidmouth*
John W.C. Pavey, *Flat 2, 1a Brownlow Road, Redhill, Surrey*
Bruce R. Peeke, *Terreta, Vicarage Road, Sidmouth*
Reg and Hilda Peirce, *Clypo, Cottington Mead, Sidmouth*
T.W. Peters, *Saltaire, Harcombe Lane, Sidford*
M.E. Philips
Eileen Pooley, *74 Malden Road, Sidmouth*
R.K. Press, *2 Woolbrook Park, Sidmouth*
Lady Preston, *Beeston Hall, Beeston St Lawrence, Norwich*
Steve and Roz Price, *15 Oxford Road, Undercliffe, Bradford*
Jocé Prosser, *Bright Waters, Sid Lane, Sidmouth*
J. Purchase, *Meadowcroft, Darnell Close, Sidmouth*

R

Carolyn Radford, *Brook Cottage, Tipton St John, Sidmouth*
Bez Raine, *3 Salcombe Villas, Salcombe Road, Sidmouth*

Anthony and Rosemary Richards, *Thorne Farm, Salcombe Regis, Nr Sidmouth*
Mrs Grace Roe, *24 Prestbury Park, Chelford Road, Prestbury, Cheshire*
Mrs P.S. Rostance, *The Griffons, Coreway, Sidford*
K.A. Rowland, *1 The Square, Middle Woolbrook, Sidmouth*
W.M. Russell, *4 Ridgeway Close, Sidbury*

S

Dr W.R. St Cin, *Long Close Cottage, Sidbury*
Mr Donald Sellek, *4 Primley Mead, Sidmouth*
Mrs Anne Settle, *late of Meadowcroft, Byes Lane, Sidford*
Sidmouth Conservative Club, *Radway, Sidmouth*
Sidmouth Town Council, *Woolcombe House, Woolcombe Lane, Sidmouth*
A.R. Stone, *15 High Meadow, Woolbrook, Sidmouth*
L.W. Stubbs *40 Powys House, All Saints Road, Sidmouth*
David Swindell, *Briar Cottage, Roselands, Sidmouth*

T

Mrs V. Tassie, *14 Goodwin Gardens, Waddon, Croydon, Surrey*
Mr and Mrs Denzil Taylor, *2 Seaton Burn, Boughmore Road, Sidmouth*
Mrs Thompson, *Harts Mead, Buckley Road, Sidbury*
Betty Thompson, *Jasmine Cottage, Sidcliffe, Sidmouth*
Mr L. and Dr R.S. Tobias, *121 Russell Road, Moseley, Birmingham*
Christopher C. Tribe, *2 Sid Vale Cottages, Sid Park Road, Sidmouth*

V

Mr G.A. Valters, *21 Primley Mead, Sidmouth*

W

Barbara E. Wall, *Lawn End, Elysian Fields, Sidmouth*
Mary E. Wallis, *2 Blackmore View, Sidmouth*
B.W. Warr, *17 Sid Lane, Sidmouth*
N. Webb, *2 Claremont, Station Road, Sidmouth*
Brian A. Websdale, *3 Linstead Court, Station Road, Sidmouth*
Eileen and Leslie R. Westcott, *Southernhay, 1a Connaught Close, Sidmouth*
Gill Whitfield, *1 Chestnut Way, Newton Poppleford, Sidmouth*
David John White, *Southfield, Griggs Lane, Fortescue, Sidmouth*
Rosalind Whitfield, *Allward, Salcombe Hill Road, Sidmouth*
Elspeth Williams, *9 Cottington Court, Sidmouth*
Mary R. Williams, *2 The Street, Cherhill, Calne, Wilts*
Michael Charles Williams, *1748 Lee Avenue, Victoria, British Columbia*
Simon James Williams
Mr J.H. Wilsher, *Riphay, Cotlands, Sidmouth*
Michael Wright, *Coln Cottage, Marston Meysey, Nr Cricklade, Swindon*
Peter and Thelma Wyatt, *35 Livonia Road, Sidmouth*

Y

Mrs Margaret Yendle, *10a Claremont Road, East Twickenham, Middlesex*
Misses B. and K. Young, *Flat 2, Roselands Court, Roselands, Sidmouth*

ACKNOWLEDGEMENTS

The following publications have been referred to:
    Rev. E. Butcher *Sidmouth Scenery and Views*
    P. O. Hutchinson *History of Sidmouth* and *Diaries*
    Anna Sutton *A Story of Sidmouth*
    Minutes of the Sid Vale Association
    Ronald Wilson *Salcombe Regis Sketches*

I would like to thank the following for their help in compiling this book: Vernon Bartlett, Mr B. Bradley, Mrs Drewe, Mrs P. Dunn, Mr R. M. D. Fisher, Mr and Mrs J. Greer, Mr Alan Hunt, Mrs S. Lane, Mr and Mrs D. J. Mortimore, Mr F. A. C. Pinney, Mrs B. Prideaux, Mr J. S. Reeder, Mrs M. Reed, Mrs P. C. Scratchley, Mrs E. Wray. Thanks are also due to the Devon Record Office for permission to reproduce the illustrations by P. O. Hutchinson.

INTRODUCTION

The aim of this book is to give, through contemporary photographs, some idea of how Sidmouth developed in the nineteenth century, to show the people who lived here during this period and to preserve some of the history of the town.

The story is built around the stock of photographs in Sidmouth Museum, most of which were collected by the late Dr Gerald Gibbens, a past Honorary Curator of the Museum and Past President of the Sid Vale Association. It has taken a long time to gather the appropriate information for the captions to the photographs and I regret any errors that may have crept in.

The period covered by the book is some one hundred years from 1800, during which time the basic layout of the town was established. Nature provided the setting in a lovely valley bounded by two beautiful hills which has prevented modern urban sprawl to the east and the west. Twentieth-century development has been along the valley and further erosion is resisted in an effort to preserve this unique small town.

Many people come here on holiday and then retire here, many others are regular visitors; to them and to all Sidmouthians I hope this book will give enjoyment and happy memories.

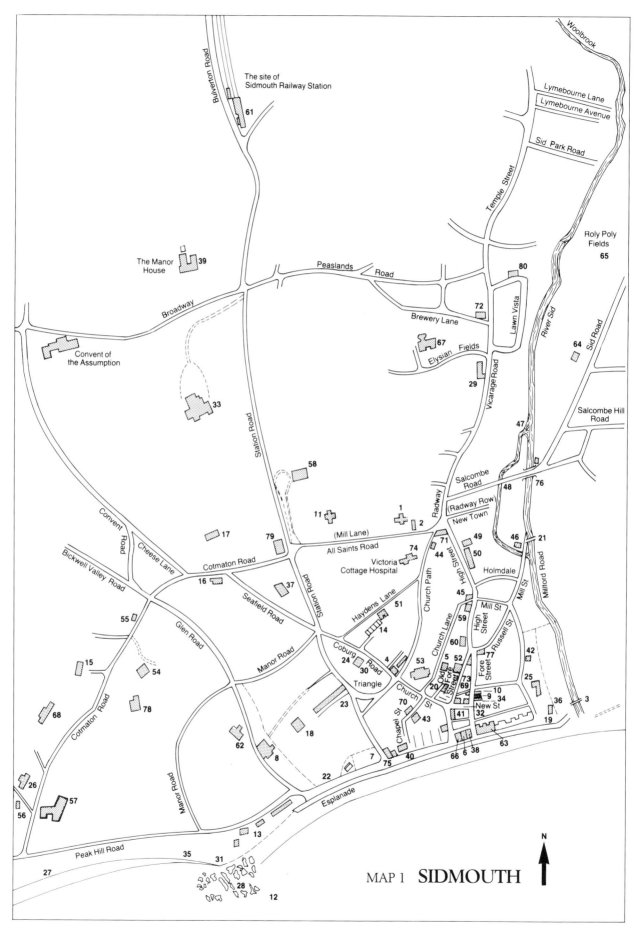

The site of
Sidmouth Railway Station

61

Bulverton Road

Woolbrook

Lymebourne Lane
Lymebourne Avenue

Sid Park Road

Temple Street

The Manor
House   39

Peaslands   Road

Broadway

Brewery Lane

80

Lawn Vista

72

Roly Poly
Fields
65

Convent of
the Assumption

67
Elysian   Fields

29

Vicarage Road

64   Sid Road

River Sid

33

Salcombe Hill
Road

Station Road

58

47

Salcombe
Road   Radway

1

11   (Mill Lane)   2

Radway Row

New Town

48   76

21

Convent Road

Cheese Lane

Bickwell Valley Road

17   79

All Saints Road   71   49
44   50

46

Cotmaton Road

16

37

Victoria
Cottage Hospital

74

High Street

Holmdale

Millford Road
Mill St

Seafield Road

Station Road

Haydens Lane

51

45   Mill St

59   High
Street

Church Path

Church Lane

Russell St

42

55

Glen Road

14

60

77

25

15

Manor Road

Coburg Road

24   30

4

53   5   52   73
Old   69
20   Fore   Street

10
9   34

36   3

54

Triangle

23

Church St

Fore Street

New St   19

68

78

Cotmaton Road

18

Chapel St

Church St
70   43   41   32

62

8

7   75   40   66   6   38   63

22

26

Manor Road

Esplanade

57

56

13

Peak Hill Road   35

31

27

28

12

MAP 1   **SIDMOUTH**

N

KEY TO MAP 1

1	All Saints' Church	56	Peak Hill Water Works
2	All Saints' School	57	Peak House
3	Alma Bridge	58	Powys
4	Amyatt's Terrace	59	Dr Pullin's House
5	Arkell's Brewery	60	Rahere House
6	Beach House	61	Railway station
7	Bedford Lawns	62	Royal Glen Hotel (Woolbrook Cottage)
8	Belmont	63	Royal York Hotel
9	Bevett's shoe shop	64	Salcombe House
10	Cash Dispensing Chemists	65	Salcombe Lodge
11	Cedar Shade (Belle Vue)	66	The Shed
12	Chit Rock	67	Sidholme (Richmond Lodge)
13	Clifton Place (Heiffer's Row)	68	Sidmouth House (The Lodge)
14	Coburg Terrace	69	Trumps
15	Cotland House	70	Tudor Cottage
16	Cotmaton House	71	Unitarian Chapel
17	Cottington	72	Vallance's Brewery
18	Cricket Pavilion	73	Veale's grocers
19	Drill Hall	74	Victoria Hospital
20	Ebdons Court	75	Wallis's Marine Library
21	Ford and bridge	76	Waterloo Bridge
22	The Fort	77	Winchesters
23	Fortfield Terrace	78	Witheby
24	Fort House	79	Woodlands
25	Gas Works	80	Woolcombe House
26	Golf Club		
27	Guns from the fort		
28	Harbour stone		
29	The Hermitage		
30	Hope Cottage (Museum)		
31	Jacob's Ladder		
32	Knight's (Cinema)		
33	Knowle (Marine Villa)		
34	Lakes omnibus offices		
35	Lime kiln		
36	Liquidizing plant		
37	Little Court Hotel (Violet Bank Cottage)		
38	London & South Western Bank (Temple House)		
39	Manor House		
40	Marine Place		
41	Market House		
42	Marsh Chapel (original site)		
43	Marsh Chapel (new site)		
44	May Cottage		
45	Methodist Chapel		
46	The mill		
47	Mill dam		
48	Mill leat		
49	Myrtle Cottage		
50	Myrtle Terrace		
51	The Old Chancel		
52	Old Ship Inn		
53	Parish church		
54	Pauntley (The Marino)		
55	Pauntley Lodge		

MAP 2 **SIDBURY**

1 Cottages in Bridge Street
2 Court Hall
3 The old bakery
4 Parish church
5 Sand

Heavy outline indicates buildings that are Listed Grade II

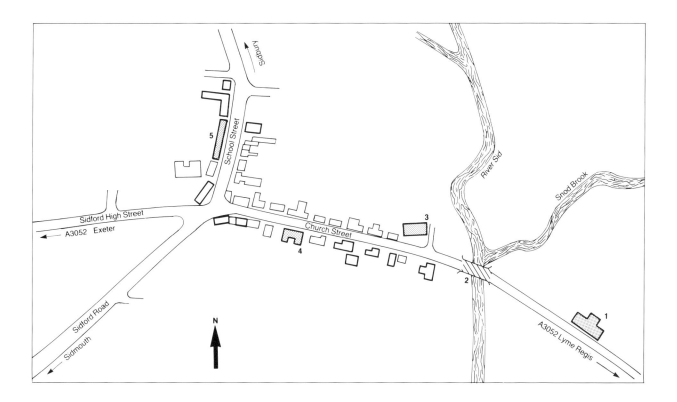

MAP 3 **SIDFORD**

1 Blue Ball Inn
2 Packhorse bridge
3 Parish church
4 Porch Cottage
5 School House

Heavy outline indicates buildings that are Listed Grade II

Views of Sidmouth from the east . . .

SIDMOUTH'S BEGINNINGS

Sidmouth, spelt Sedemuda in Domesday, lies in the middle of the coastline of Lyme Bay, bounded on the east by Portland Bill and on the west by Start Point. It is situated where the River Sid runs through an attractive valley, with Salcombe Hill to the east and Peak Hill to the west. The hills are flat-topped, rising from 500 feet to over 800 feet at the head of the 5-mile-long valley.

In 1789 William Day produced a map of the manor. The population at that time was approximately 1240.

Local farming was done on the open field system originally introduced by the Saxons. Lands were divided into strips, bounded not by hedges but by the ploughing of drainage channels. Each farmer would have strips of half an acre in three or more fields. This

. . . and the west.

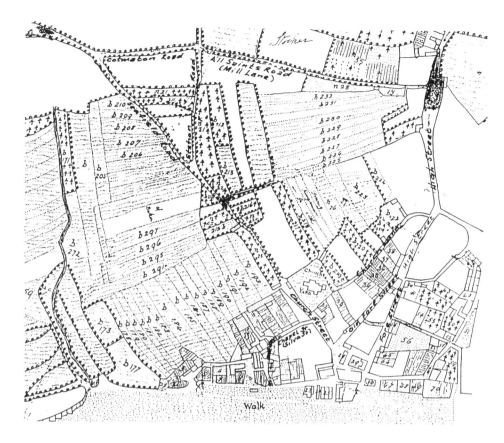

method gave a fairer distribution of good soil, poorly drained land, moor and waste land and also allowed for one field to be left fallow for a season. This was sound economics when each man tried to grow enough to feed his own family, and the villagers had a shared interest in the land although it still belonged to the Lord of the Manor.

For many years before 1800, Sidmouth was a small fishing village. Most of the buildings, with few exceptions, were constructed of cob on stone foundations, with thatched roofs. In those days, the main occupations of the inhabitants were fishing and lace making. The following photographs show some of the old cob cottages in Sidmouth.

Cottages in the High Street in front of Pikes Court.

14

Cottages in Pikes Court which were demolished in 1932.

Cottages in High Street.

Church Street in 1849.

Fisherman's cottage.

Cottage at Middle Woolbrook, built in 1693.

Grand Houses

There are several very old houses in Sidmouth. One such is **Old Hayes** in Station Road which was built in medieval times. It is recorded that Sir William Peryam was granted the manor by Queen Elizabeth I in 1598, and he lived there for a short time.

In 1809, Lord Gwydir bought Old Hayes. He subsequently converted and enlarged it. George IV, when Prince of Wales, lived at Old Hayes with Lord Gwydir for a short time.

The name of the house was later changed from Old Hayes to **Woodlands.** In 1856 a Mr Johnson owned the house and replaced the thatch with expensive hand-cut hexagonal roof tiles. He had the stonework for the gables prepared in Italy and shipped to England. The stonework was pegged to the gables with oaken pegs. Woodlands opened its doors to paying guests in 1918.

Woodlands after Lord Gwydir, about 1828.

16

Woodlands after Mr Johnson, late nineteenth century.

The original **Cotmaton House** *(Cotmaton Road)* dated from medieval times. During alterations in the nineteenth century a stone was revealed which showed the date 1520. In the late eighteenth century the Carslake family lived there. John Carslake built a new Cotmaton House in about 1809, next to the original house.

The 'new' Cotmaton House, with the original medieval house behind.

17

1950

Above: Cotmaton House at around 1950.

Left:
The drinking fountain in Cotmaton Road, opposite the house. The original fountain, 'The Lion's Mouth', was installed by the Carslakes in 1835. The Parish Council replaced it with a new fountain in 1860.

The main growth of Sidmouth did not occur until almost the end of the eighteenth century. The western side of the Sid valley was devoid of houses until 1793 when Emanuel Baruch Lousada bought Peak Tenement and 125 acres, and built the first **Peak House.** This was unfortunately burnt down and the second Peak House was built by Sir Thomas Dewey in 1904. This house still exists today.

18

The first Peak House, photographed in 1870.

The present Peak House *(Peak Hill Road/Cotmaton Road)*.

Fortfield Terrace was commissioned and built by Thomas Jenkins, the Lord of the Manor, between 1790 and 1795. He engaged a young Polish architect called Novosielski to design and build a fine terrace facing the sea, but set back behind a field. Novosielski had been born in Rome in 1760, and it was in Rome that he carried out his architectural studies. Unfortunately, Novosielski fell ill and died before the building work had been finished, and the terrace was therefore never completed. In architectural terms this is a pity, but it is possible that had the terrace been finished as planned, Sidmouth would not have had the beautiful cricket ground that it has today.

The terrace has had some interesting and important tenants in its time. These include the Grand Duchess Helena, sister-in-law to the Czar of Russia; Lord Gwydir, Lord High Chamberlain to the Prince Regent; Lady Le Despenser, whose husband built Knowle; and Edward Barrett who, compelled by financial difficulties, sold his estate in Herefordshire and brought Elizabeth and the family to Sidmouth. They stayed at Fortfield Terrace for one year before moving to Cedar Shade in Mill Lane.

The building of the terrace saw the real beginning of Sidmouth's development. It attracted the nobility and gentry to the town who were able to build very pleasing cottages and houses of individual design.

Fortfield Terrace when it was first built had no balconies and part of it was built in red brick.

Below:
A later view of Fortfield Terrace when the balconies had been added and the whole terrace faced.

A friendly cricket match between 'Visitors' and 'Residents' on Fortfield in 1868. The building on the left of the picture was originally built as three houses in 1820. It is now the Torbay Hotel. To the right of the picture are the Sussex Hotel and the Bedford Hotel.

Sports on the cricket field in 1894.

Knowle *(Station Road)* was originally known as **Marine Villa.** At around 1809 or 1810, Lord Le Despenser was engaged in building Knowle Cottage. It was to be in the form of a quadrangle containing about forty rooms. Some time after it was finished, it was rented by the Marquis of Bute. By 1821 it was owned by a Mr Fish, who made a vast collection of objects, mainly of plate, jewellery and works of art. Also between 1821 and 1841 he added exotic plants, animals, birds and fish to his collection and on fine Mondays he would admit members of the public to see them. Mr Fish died in London in 1861, and in 1865 the house passed to the Thorntons. Mr R. N. Thornton, an excellent cricketer at Oxford, took over the house. He leased Fortfield for 14 years and brought the ground to fine condition.

During its history, Knowle has been considerably altered as can be seen from the following pictures. The house became a hotel in 1880, when even more alterations were carried out. In 1974, the house became the offices of East Devon District Council.

Knowle when it was owned by Mr Fish in 1821.

Some of the extensive alterations to Knowle.

The Knowle Hotel after 1880.

Cotland House *(Cotmaton Road)*. Thomazine, wife of John Carslake, laid the foundation stone of a house he was building in January 1818. This house was Cotland House. The family did not always reside there – it was sometimes let. Since the Second World War the house has been demolished and a cul-de-sac of bungalows built.

Sketch by George Rowe of Cotland House in 1826.

Cotland House with an extension added.

Witheby *(Cotmaton Road)* was built by Mrs Powys Floyd between 1800 and 1810, but it was sold to Miss Wright before 1818. It later belonged to Mr Cunningham, a rich West Indian merchant from Bristol. On his death, the house was sold to Mr Cave, a banker and father of the Rt Hon. Stephen Cave, MP, in 1880. After the Second World War the house was demolished and replaced by modern flats.

Witheby in about 1850.

After selling Witheby, Mrs Powys Floyd built **Powys Cottage** *(All Saints Road)* between 1819 and 1826. It was a type of bungalow, with its middle section consisting of a conservatory. After the death of Mrs Powys Floyd, the house passed to her nephew Sir John Floyd, Bart. An upper floor was added with a thatched roof. This was later replaced with slates.

Below: The original Powys Cottage.

Bottom: Powys Cottage after the alterations.

Cottington.

Cottington (*Cotmaton Road*) was originally known as **Liberty Hall** and was built around 1820. It has also been known as **Springfield.** In 1880 it was bought by the Convent of the Assumption, a French educational order of nuns. Their church services were open to the public. The nuns eventually left to move to a new convent, now known as St John's School.

Cottington was subsequently owned by a Major Berkeley Levett, CVO, a Brigade Major in the Greys from 1914 to 1918. He moved into the house in 1920.

It was Major Berkeley Levett's enthusiasm for the town that brought the Duke of Connaught to Sidmouth.

After the Second World War, Cottington was demolished and Sidmouth's first block of flats was built in its place. This is called Cottington Court.

Sidmouth House (*Cotmaton Road*) was at one time known as **The Lodge.** It was built in 1810 and was the residence of Edward Lee for some years

Sidmouth House.

Sidholme (Elysian Fields/Vicarage Road) was originally called **Richmond Lodge.** It was built in 1826, in the style of a gothicized villa, for the Earl of Buckinghamshire. In 1848, following a disagreement between the countess and the local vicar, a music room was added to the house in which religious services could be held. The music room had a very fine interior, neo-classical in style with some rococo.

In 1876, Richmond Lodge became the property of Benjamin Davidson. He married Olga Noble to whom the house passed when Benjamin died in 1878. In 1884, Olga married Adolphus Frederick Lindemann, a scientist, and they had four sons and a daughter. The second son, Frederick Alexander, was the famous scientist who became a public figure as Lord Cherwell, scientific adviser to Winston Churchill during the Second World War.

In 1931, Sidholme was sold to the Wesley Guild Holiday Organization. It is now one of nine Methodist Guild Holiday Centres.

The original Richmond Lodge was built in 1826. The new entrance and music room, which were built on to the left-hand side of the house in 1848, form the present front elevation.

The original front elevation of Sidholme with the front door which now leads to the gardens.

Pauntley.

Pauntley *(Cotmaton Road)*, a beautiful Georgian house, was originally named **The Marino.** It was lived in by a Major Hicks who was renowned for his drawings and happy caricatures of the society of his day (late nineteenth century).

In 1923, the Whittington family moved to The Marino and changed the name of the house to Pauntley, after the Gloucestershire village of Pauntley where they had lived. The family were direct descendants of the famous Dick Whittington, the thrice Lord Mayor of London. Later, Pauntley became the property of Viscount and Lady Hambleden whose family founded W.H. Smith & Sons.

Before the Second World War, the house was taken over by evacuees. Children from the East End of London arrived wearing large labels. Pauntley was the first big house to be turned into a hostel for evacuees, with a matron, and communal catering arrangements. Also, in October 1940, Pauntley was the first house in the county to have a nursery centre for toddlers. This enabled their mothers to go to work. The land around Pauntley was turned into allotments.

After the war, Lord Hambleden presented Pauntley Lodge to the town, on condition that his chauffeur Mr Harry Balch and his wife could continue to live there as long as they wished. Pauntley Lodge must surely be the most desirable council house in the whole country!

Pauntley Lodge.

THE COURSE
OF THE RIVER SID

The **River Sid** rises in Pin Hill Wood to the north of Sidmouth and flows southwards down the Sid valley. The river passes through **Sidbury** – a village which has existed since Celtic times. In the latter part of the seventh century it was taken by the Saxons who built the church and probably laid out the pattern of the lanes much as they are today. Construction and reconstruction of the church continued from 1150 to 1450. In 1843 and 1884 the upper stages of the tower were accurately rebuilt.

Some of the buildings in Sidbury date back to the sixteenth and seventeenth centuries, but most are of eighteenth- and nineteenth-century origin. A number of the cottages in Bridge Street are constructed of cob on stone footings and roofed with thatch.

Sidbury church in the 1800s.

Left: A later picture of the church showing the battlements and small spire.

Above: Cottages in Bridge Street.

Below: Sidbury's old bakery.

Above:
Court Hall is thought to date from the late sixteenth or early seventeenth century, with other additions incorporated in the building later. The Hall is said to have got its name from the time when the judges stayed there on their circuit rounds. It is possible that Judge Jeffreys may have stayed there.

Below:
Sand is located to the north of Sidbury. The estate dates back to some time between 1231 and 1250, during the reign of Henry III. The house became the property of the Huyshe family in 1560–61 and is still occupied by the same family. Sand was rebuilt in 1594, and it is this building that stands today. It is open to the public at certain times of year.

Sidford is located where the River Sid is joined by the Snodbrook before it flows southwards. The stone packhorse bridge at Sidford was built during the twelfth century at the time when Salcombe stone was being sent to Exeter to build the cathedral. The ford here was very stony and it is thought that the bridge was built to lessen the risk of laden packhorses slipping. When the bridge was widened in 1930, a plaque was inserted stating that the original bridge had been left untouched.

Sidford packhorse bridge in 1860.

Sidford Bridge some time after 1868 – the date the parish church was built.

Dr Gerald Gibbens, a past curator of Sidmouth Museum, walks over the old packhorse bridge.

Sidford consists of many cob and thatch cottages built on stone foundations, dating from the eighteenth and nineteenth centuries. Some cottages are somewhat older, such as **Porch Cottage.** This was built in 1574 and legend has it that King Charles II slept there during his escape after the Battle of Worcester. This picture of Porch Cottage is by Peter Orlando Hutchinson and dates from 1855.

Left:
Another P.O. Hutchinson watercolour of School Street in Sidford. The school house was in the centre of this row of cottages which remain intact today. Their most outstanding features are their stone chimneys which date from the Stuart period. One bears the date 1633 and another 1641.

Below:
The **Blue Ball Inn** in Sidford is a fine cob and thatch building which dates back to 1385. It is little changed on the outside and the inside has been tastefully decorated. The inn has been run by the same family since 1912.

Above:
The River Sid continues to flow southwards into Sidmouth and this view looks upstream towards **Sidcliffe**.

Below:
The River Sid flows by the 'Roly-poly Fields', seen on the right. This view northwards shows Salters Meadow and Sid Park on the left.

Right:
The River Sid is also joined by the Woolbrook along its course near **Lymebourne.**

Salcombe Lodge *(Sid Road)* was built in 1810 and is considered to be one of the best examples of Regency Gothic architecture. The front elevation is a delight, displaying nine curved pointed windows and an arched doorway.

Salcombe House *(Sid Road)* is now Hunter's Moon Hotel. It was built in the late part of the eighteenth century by Mrs Brutton. In 1810 the Rev. William Jenkins resided there, his vicarage being let as a lodging house.

Later the lease passed to Sir W. Coburn, absentee Dean of York, and then in about 1841, to Charles Cornish.

Sir William Coburn, whose first wife was a daughter of Sir Robert Peel, became Dean of York, but in 1841 he was deprived of his living on a charge of simony. An appeal to the Court of Queen's Bench did not secure a reversal of the judgement, but prohibited it from being carried into effect. It is thought that there was influence from Sir Robert Peel. Other stories about the Dean are recorded in Peter Orlando Hutchinson's *History*.

It is said that the Dean was the first man in the valley to be seen carrying an umbrella.

Salcombe Lodge

Salcombe House

The Mill Dam with the entrance to the mill leat.

The **Mill Dam** was built in 1801 to feed a man-made leat which took water through to the mill near the ford. This particular dam was washed away. In 1884 a new dam was constructed using 12-inch deal baulks. These were laid across the river to a height of 5 feet. The water flowed into the mill leat – the surplus ran over the top of the wooden baulks and down the steps on the other side which were 5 to 6 feet long and composed of fir poles laid close together, parallel with the flow of the stream. The mill leat, once it left the mill, eventually rejoined the river.

Looking upstream towards the steps of the dam.

Left:
The mill leat ran below Salcombe Road. This has since been
filled in.

Below: An old print of the mill by the ford in Mill Street.

Waterloo Bridge *(Salcombe Road)* was constructed in stone in 1817 to take the new Salcombe road from Radway over the River Sid. A toll-house and toll-gate were erected alongside to pay for the new road.

Above: The bridge and the toll-house.

Below: The toll-gate on Waterloo Bridge.

Alma Bridge *(The Ham)* has an interesting history. After much pressure over nine years by the Sid Vale Association, it was in 1855 that Mrs Cornish, wife of the Lord of the Manor of Salcombe Regis, finally consented to the building of a bridge over the river which would shorten the walk from Sidmouth to Salcombe Regis. The bridge was named after the battle of Alma in 1854. It was originally constructed from timbers of the recently wrecked ship, the *Laurel*. The bridge was 125 feet long, 2 feet wide and stood 8 feet above the river. It had five pairs of supports and a 3-foot hand rail. The total cost of building the timber bridge was £26.10s.

In 1877, Alma Bridge was damaged in a severe storm and the repairs cost £34. The bridge was, however, of poor construction and a new bridge was built by the Urban District Council in 1900. It was completely renovated in 1986.

Above: The first Alma Bridge under construction in 1855.

Left: The completed Alma Bridge.

Construction of the second bridge in 1900.

The second Alma Bridge completed.

Salcombe Regis

At this point we will take the opportunity to go 'up over', as they said in times past, to the village of Salcombe Regis.

The name 'Salcombe' is derived from the salt works that used to exist at the mouth of the Combe and 'Regis' commemorates the fact of the Manor having been granted to the Church of Exeter by King Athelstan (925–940).

The village is dominated by the lovely **Church of St Mary and St Peter.** A small wooden church may have stood here; in Norman times this was replaced by a stone building during the reign of Stephen (1135–1154). Other additions were made in 1150.

In the thirteenth century there were extensions and additions when the church was dedicated by Bishop Bronscombe to the Blessed Virgin Mary. In about 1450, the tower was built and extensive alterations were made by Bishop Lacey, and the whole edifice was dedicated to St Peter. (Simultaneously stone from the same quarry was being shipped or taken by packhorse to Exeter for building the Cathedral.)

There are three bells in the tower; the treble of medieval date was cast in Exeter about 1432, the second bell and the tenor were recast in 1633 and 1637 respectively. They were rehung and a new cage was made for them in 1887, when a clock was put in the tower, the whole forming a Queen's Jubilee memorial; the chiming apparatus was added in 1897.

Restoration of the church was begun in 1849 and again in 1869.

Thorn Farm, the demesne farm of the Dean and Chapter and seat of the manor courts, has some pre-Reformation details. It was the homestead of the stewards of the manor, Hopper and Clapp, till the latter years of the eighteenth century. Since then it has been a farmhouse.

At the road junction, fifty yards above the farm, stands the Salcombe Thorn. A thorn tree has been maintained there from Saxon times, if not earlier. It marks the boundary between the cultivated fields of the combe and the open common. It is believed that this was a primitive folk-moot.

Above: Thorn Farm

Right: Slade Farm

Slade Farm copyhold was acquired by William Leigh. He prospered and was able to build a fine new farmhouse in 1771 and to buy the freehold from the Dean and Chapter. He must have been aware that his premises were used by smugglers.

His daughter married John Carslake of Cotmaton, Sidmouth. Their daughter, Thomazine, married Samuel Woodett Browne. The Brownes had two daughters, Annie and Thomazine. After her first husband died, Thomazine married Sir Norman Lockyer, who built the Observatory on Salcombe Hill. Annie Leigh Browne was prominent in Sidmouth (see p. 105).

Slade Farm became a home for aged donkeys in 1975 and is now known as the Donkey Sanctuary.

Above:
The River Sid at the estuary.

The river where it passes
through the shingle to reach
the sea.

To call the last part of the River Sid an estuary is something of a misnomer. The shingle bar at the end of the river causes the flow of water to pass *through* the shingle for most days of the year – usually when the rainfall is low. However, back in the early fifteenth century there was a harbour at the mouth of the river. But it is thought that a spell of stormy weather, combined with a sudden land rise, caused this and other south coast harbours to become blocked. In the winter when the rainfall is heavy, the river cuts several small channels through the shingle into the sea.

Sidmouth's Harbour

At the beginning of the nineteenth century, a scheme was proposed to build a new harbour at the mouth of the river. In 1810, estimates were prepared for the building of a harbour at the Ham, and in 1825 at Chit Rock. But by 1830, both schemes had been abandoned. In 1836, however, an Act was passed for a Chit Rock harbour. A new company was formed to carry out the work, which was to be completed in seven years.

It was decided that the best way to get stone for the construction of the harbour was to use a railway running eastwards to Hook Ebb (where the stone was to come from). The railway was laid from Chit Rock by the side of the Esplanade, eastwards over the river by a viaduct, through a ⅓-mile-long tunnel at Pennington Point, to Hook Ebb – a distance of 1½ miles. The entrance to the tunnel can clearly be seen in the photograph opposite.

The viaduct over the river was constructed of ninety-one pairs of wooden piles driven into the river bed to support the wooden beams which were to carry the rails. The total span of the viaduct was 425 feet. The remains of one of the piles can be seen in Sidmouth Museum, kindly presented by Mr Longbottom of Salcombe Regis.

A local blacksmith named Coles was commissioned to make a machine to transport the stone. However, his machine was worked manually and did not have enough power to pull the weight of the stone. A steam engine was sent for as an alternative. It arrived in the town to a great deal of cheering and flag waving and was placed on the rails. Then disaster struck – it would not go through the tunnel! Not to be totally wasted, the steam engine was 'yoked' to a few carriages and trips were made up and down the Esplanade. By 1837, all the money to build the harbour had gone – the harbour had not even been started. By 1838, the engine and construction tools had also gone and the piles of the viaduct sawn off. The first and only stone which was brought for the harbour had been transported by sea. It can still be seen on the beach today.

The first and only stone brought for the harbour.

Flooding

Flooding of the river was quite common at one time, especially near the ford. In 1795 the only crossing point on the river was formed by a tree trunk. When the water level was high, debris would collect behind the tree and block the river, causing it to flow down Mill Street into Eastern Town. Even when the tree was replaced by a low bridge, similar flooding problems occurred. After more flooding the bed of the river was lowered and stone walls were built along its banks. A new higher bridge was built and the flooding problem has been alleviated. A heavy storm in the winter of 1989 caused the river to rise and a small number of domestic properties on the east bank in Millford Road were flooded. But the improvements prevented flood water entering the town.

... around the toll-house ...

Flooding in 1960 at Millford Road ...

... in Mill Street.

Damage to the bridge at the ford.

The River Sid bursts its banks.

THE RIVER AND SEAFRONT AREA

Marsh Chapel was erected on The Ham in 1810. As Nonconformists, the Barrett family attended the chapel for several years and it was here that Elizabeth Barrett formed a romantic association with the minister, George B. Hunter, in 1832.

Sometime before 1841 it was decided that Marsh Chapel was not in a very convenient situation, and as the lease was about to expire, a new site was sought. Some land in Silva Street, Western Town (now Chapel Street) was purchased and a new chapel erected and opened in 1846.

Right: An artist's reconstruction of the old Marsh Chapel.

The original Marsh Chapel on The Ham (extreme right).

The replacement chapel in Chapel Street.

In 1870, work started on a liquidizing plant on **The Ham.** It was to have an underground sewage tank and an elongated sea outfall pipe. The plant should have been completed by the winter of 1870, but owing to problems in the planning, delays occurred causing the tank to be left open all through the summer, and the outfall pipe was not finished until the winter months. A great deal of discontent in the town also occurred because the workforce had been brought in from outside the area.

The Ham was given to the town in 1896 by Mr Radford, a local solicitor who also owned Hope Cottage (now the museum). One of the conditions under which he gave the land to the town was that it remained untouched and left for recreation. Later, in 1899, he was very upset to find how badly The Ham had been disfigured through the installation of the sewer pipes and drains, and the gas works. But towards the end of the nineteenth century, local unemployed fishermen were employed by the council to raise the level of The Ham meadow. The ground was levelled and grass, flowers and seats provided for the public. A belt of trees was planted to hide the gas works.

The installation of the sewage and drainage pipes was spread over some years, some even being relaid. After the initial stage up to 1899, the process then continued more slowly as the town developed.

The underground tank under construction in 1870.

In 1873, a Mr Dunning came from Middlesbrough and bought up the original gas works which existed at Water Lane, Winslade. This was closed when Mr Dunning purchased a large part of The Ham and built a new gas works there in 1875. He used shingle from the beach to make the concrete. He also had a plan to construct a jetty alongside which the coal ships could offload their cargoes into railway trucks. These would then transport the coal straight to the gas works. His first jetty was blown down and for 5 years he attempted to reinstate it, but eventually the money ran out. The gas works continued to operate for many years until they were moved to the station. Now even those gas works have gone. When the works moved from The Ham, the scenery and environment of the area was greatly improved.

The Ham before the development of the gas works.

The gas works on The Ham.

The Drill Hall on The Ham was built in 1895. The site was presented to the town by Mr Radford.

50

The Esplanade in Sidmouth has a long and interesting history. The first attempt at creating a promenade along the sea front was in 1805 when a rolled and flattened earth bank was constructed. This was not very successful as it failed to keep the sea at bay and consequently the town was often flooded.

The Esplanade as a rolled earth bank.

Chit Rock, to the west of the sea front, was destroyed in a violent storm in 1824. A report of the time gives a vivid picture of the occurrences on that stormy night:

'As the tide rose after midnight, the wind increased in violence and assisted by this violence speedily threw the huge billows over the Esplanade [which at that time was only a bank of earth and shingle]. The waves rushed down the alleyways and openings, through the houses and occupied all the lower parts of the town. The inhabitants were awakened by the noise of rushing water, the breaking of doors and windows which let the tide into the houses, the noise of falling chimneys and flying slates. In a drapers shop the water had risen over the counter ruining silks, woollens, lace, gloves and ribbons; the damage was over £1,000 [which was a considerable sum in 1824].

The fishermen were rowing their boats along Old Fore Street, Fore Street and New Street rescuing people in their nightwear. When the tide had turned and the beach could be reached, it was realised the Chit Rock was no longer to be seen. The old mass of rock had been knocked over in the night. The rock which had stood the storms of years was swept away in an instant so strong was the storm.'

The rock was particularly missed by the fishermen. It was the first thing they sought when returning to land as it gave them their bearings and told them exactly where they were.

The Chit Rock.

52

The first Esplanade looking east ...

The first permanent Esplanade was built at a cost of £2000 in 1837 and stretched from The Ham to Fort House. The whole aspect of the shore was changed by the disappearance of the shingle, caused by the action of the tide and by people removing it for building work. The resulting pressure of the sea on the wall was considerable and through a lack of maintenance, the wall began to crumble. Holes appeared in the Esplanade's foundations from time to time, but were ignored by the Local Board through the 1870s and 1880s. Instead they chose to repair damage to the Esplanade's surface. In November 1923 a large hole appeared in the Esplanade which was temporarily repaired. This was followed three weeks later by another hole which let the sea through to the town and caused flooding. Once again the holes were repaired, but in the winter of 1923 the wall broke down again and the town flooded once more. In the following year, a severe storm caused the sea to demolish great lengths of the Esplanade. As a result, a new Esplanade was built and opened in 1926.

... and west.

The storm damage in 1924.

Above: Construction of the new sea wall.

PROGRAMME OF

Sidmouth Sea Wall Opening Ceremony.

MARCH 20th, 1926.

Col. The Rt Hon. Wilfrid Ashley MP cuts the tape and opens
the new sea wall.

Left:
The programme of events at the opening of the sea wall in
1926.

York Terrace was built in 1810 on a site where there once stood a shipyard which built ships for the Newfoundland fishery. In 1885, an old fisherman, Thomas Heiffer of Heiffer's Row (see p. 67), said that he could remember as a boy seeing two vessels on the stocks at the same time. The ships were launched over the ridge (now the Esplanade) and their rigging and fitting out completed in the shelter of Exmouth harbour.

In 1887, to commemorate Queen Victoria's Jubilee, Mr Rogers, the Proprietor of the Royal York Hotel (Nos 1 and 2 York Terrace) invited the local fishermen to attend the Vaults for a pint of beer and refreshments in honour of the Queen. P.O. Hutchinson recalls in his diaries that the Second Devon Artillery Volunteers used to meet at the Royal York Hotel.

No. 4 York Terrace was at one time Marsh's Assembly Room. In 1851 it had been fitted out to accommodate lectures, parties, balls and auction sales. No. 5 York Terrace was, in 1851, Butters' Baths. Here one could get 'warm, cold and showerbaths at any hour of the day'. The rest of the houses in York Terrace were lodging houses. The yard at the end of the terrace was used by Mr John Potbury for storing coal. The yard was later owned by Miller & Lilley. At the end of the yard stood the old lifeboat house. In 1900 Mr James Pepperell bought part of the yard and built Shenstone in 1911. Later, the historian Anna Sutton's husband Ernest built Carlton Mansions on this site in 1923, the first flats in Sidmouth.

The Royal York Hotel in about 1850.

The London & South Western Bank (*Fore Street and Esplanade*) building was originally known as **Temple House**. The bank began trading at Mr Radford's office, Hope Cottage, and moved to Temple House in 1876. Much later the bank became Barclays Bank. It is recorded that a bank existed in the Market Place many years earlier in around 1811, when a Sidmouth pound note was issued.

Facsimile of a Sidmouth £1 note.

Sidmouth's bank (on the extreme left).

Beach House as a two-storey building is the second house on the right.

Beach House (*Esplanade*) was built in 1795 and is a Regency jewel. It is one of the earliest houses on the Esplanade. In 1810 it was 'a lounging place in a conspicuous and pleasant situation'. It was later known as Blossom House and then when it became the property of J. G. King, Esq. it was renamed Beach House. Until approximately 1839 the house consisted of ground and first floors only. After 1839 a third storey was added.

Beach House with the third storey added.

Before 1800, the building known as **The Shed**, situated to the west of Beach House, was in rather poor condition. However, early in the nineteenth century it is shown as a neat construction of planed wood, painted white, handsomely glazed at the western end and thatched. The Shed had been rebuilt in about 1809. On the ground floor there were benches all around which gave a good view of the sea. It was ornamented with stone columns which supported the first floor. This housed a billiard room with an excellent table. The Shed soon became a favourite retreat for visitors who could lounge, chat and admire the views of the coast. Today it is known as The Mocha, but its purpose has changed little – it is a coffee and tea house. The Shed was originally opened by John Wallis who made quite a success of the place. He later moved to another site further west in the town (see p.61).

The Shed.

Marine Place (*Esplanade*) was a row of lodging houses built in 1820. They were later pulled down and re-built as apartments. This building was subsequently developed into the Riviera Hotel.

Marine Place lodging houses.

Marine Place rebuilt as apartments.

60

On 20 June 1809, John Wallis moved from The Shed and built a new library known as **Wallis's Marine Library**. It was established under the patronage of Lord Gwydir, Lady Willoughby, Lord and Lady Le Despenser and Emanuel Baruch Lousada. This establishment was long awaited in Sidmouth. It was a place where people could lounge and discuss the news, and chat and gossip together. The library was well supplied each day with the London and provincial newspapers as well as some of the more popular periodical publications. Educational books, sectional maps and a circulating library completed the establishment. In 1815 HMS *Bellerophon* passed this way with Napoleon on board. All the hire telescopes at the Library were taken. Napoleon was transferred to HMS *Northumberland* at Torbay and taken to St Helena. Between 1815 and 1845 the building was enlarged, and by 1865 had become the Bedford Hotel.

Top right: John Wallis's new library, 1809–10.

Right: The library after enlargement.

The building as the Bedford Hotel in the late nineteenth century. To the left are three houses which later became the Torbay Hotel. The land opposite the Bedford Hotel was known as Bedford Lawns.

In 1908, **Bedford Lawns** (*Esplanade*) was levelled when it was proposed during that season that bowls could be played on it. This saw the beginnings of the bowls club as an offshoot of the cricket club.

Activities apparently ceased during the First World War and the lawns were inundated with sea water during winter storms. This obviously destroyed the bowling green. In the early 1920s, the council decided that Coburg Fields could be used for bowls and tennis, and Bedford Lawns were abandoned. The land is now used as a car park, but there is a covenant still in existence that states that it should not be built on.

The first Easter handout of hot-cross buns and oranges on Bedford Lawns. It is recorded that in 1898 buns were given to the children of the parish. The custom must have lapsed because in 1930 it was reintroduced and still continues today.

Sidmouth's Fort. In 1628 the Privy Council suggested that Sidmouth should have its own fort in order to protect itself. It is not certain when the fort was built but there are occasional references to powder and shot being ordered for the ordnance there.

In 1794, there was rumour of a French invasion. Sidmouth raised eighty men as a local force to man the battery at Fortfield, which consisted of four twelve-pounder guns and a six-pounder field gun.

After the Battle of Waterloo in 1815, the fort was abandoned. Two of the guns were used to prop up the church belfry and the other two were used as gateposts at a builder's yard at the eastern end of the Esplanade. In 1859 the threat of a French invasion was again apparent. In August of that year a meeting was called and fifty volunteers were required to man the defences. They were named the Second Devon Artillery Volunteers and the enrolment took place at the Town Hall on Thursday 29 September 1859. On 25 November 1859 two twenty-four-pounder guns arrived in the Market Place. The Volunteers marched down with the guns. They formed into two divisions – one in front of the wagons and one behind – and marched to Fortfield and over to the boundary facing the sea. The volunteers were then instructed how to load and fire the guns. Following the arrival of the guns the Volunteers carried out a great deal of drilling and practice, but the guns were only ever fired for the Queen's birthday. They fired off a twenty-one gun salute – the delay between each firing was one minute, but it all went well. Afterwards the officers and the men all went to the Royal York Hotel to quench their thirst. The guns were eventually moved to Peak Hill in about 1870.

A drawing by P. O. Hutchinson of how the fort might have looked in 1697. He drew this from the memory of the Sexton of Sidmouth before the guns were removed some time after 1815.

The guns on Peak Hill about 1870.

Belmont (*Esplanade*) was built as a private residence for Major Barnes in 1817, on land adjoining Fortfield. In 1818 it became the property of Sir Joseph Scott who made many improvements to the building. Sir Joseph was very involved in the town at that time. He was chairman of the committee that discussed the proposal to build a harbour at The Ham in 1812. In the same year he sat on the committee which supported Dr Bell's School (which was located in one of the houses in Amyatt's Terrace), with voluntary subscriptions. This school was well supported and denominated Sidmouth School for Education of the Infant Poor, in the principles of the established church and according to Dr Bell's plan.

Belmont was later owned by the Hina-Haycocks who in 1881 purchased the parish church organ and presented it to All Saints' Church. Following the Hina-Haycocks, Belmont passed to Mr and Mrs R. H. Wood. They advanced the money for the construction of the Drill Hall in 1895 and later presented the deeds of the building to the Rifle Volunteer Company which was formed in 1883, wiping out the £600 construction bill. Mr and Mrs Wood also gave the town a new fire engine in 1902 (see p. 119).

In 1920 Belmont was bought and enlarged by Mr Fitzgerald. He converted it into a luxury hotel, retaining much of the house's old world beauty.

The original Belmont House.

The Belmont Hotel in the 1920s.

Sidmouth's Cricket Club (*Fortfield*). In 1823, the 'Gentlemen of Sidmouth' certainly knew what they were doing when they chose Fortfield as the site for their new cricket club. The field was fenced off with iron railings and a clubhouse built with a thatched roof. However, the clubhouse fell into decay after one or two of the older members of the club died. Eventually the clubhouse was demolished sometime before 1840. It was in 1865 that Mr R. N. Thornton came to live at Knowle. He was a very keen cricketer and got the club going again. He leased Fortfield for fourteen years and got the ground into fine condition, with a proper fence around to create a cricket ground. His son, the Rev. R. T. Thornton, carried on the good work. By mowing and rolling, the ground was kept in first class condition. The public were also prevented from walking on the ground. In August 1875, following a match there between the Gentlemen of Devon and the Gentlemen of Somerset, it was decided that Somerset should play regular County matches. In 1879 the pavilion was rebuilt, forming the basis for the pavilion which stands today.

In 1881 a **Tennis Club** was formed, followed in 1907 by a **Croquet Club.**

Below: There have been many cricket teams in the club's history, but this one is with Colonel Balfour, the Lord of the Manor. *Standing, left to right:* H. Wood, G. F. Prideaux, A. Wright, F. C. Hopwood, C. Colbourne, G. B. Carter, J. A. G. Smith, Col. J. E. H. Balfour, L. Hucker, F. H. Carroll, W. Leask, E. P. Mills, W. J. Hillman, E. Purchase, W. Godfrey; *sitting, left to right:* L. Badcock, H. C. Tate, F. H. Baker, W. A. Fish (Captain), S. Tomlinson, H. E. Goodwin (Chairman), J. A. Fish, A. E. Lynham, S. A. Bartlett, R. Wadham, A. G. Leask, G. R. Fisher.

The thatched pavilion. (Earlier pavilions can be seen in the photographs on p.21.)

Above: To celebrate the 150th anniversary of Sidmouth Cricket Club, a special costumed match was held in 1973. All the players wore cricket outfits from the 1820s.

Woolbrook Cottage is now known as the Royal Glen Hotel. It was built by Mr King in 1809 and originally called King's Cottage. Just before Christmas 1819, the Duke and Duchess of Kent came with their seven-month-old daughter, Princess Victoria, to Woolbrook Cottage which was placed at their disposal by General Baynes (who had renamed the cottage). The royal visit was unhappily cut short, however, as the Duke became ill. He had been caught out in the rain and his boots became thoroughly soaked. He refused to change out of the boots because he wanted to play with his daughter. He caught a heavy cold which developed into inflammation of the lungs and the Duke died on Sunday 23 January 1820. After briefly lying in state, the Duke's body was buried at Frogmore.

The family had stayed in Sidmouth for 7 weeks, but Victoria was never to return to Sidmouth. Instead she dedicated the west window in the parish church to the memory of her father in 1864. In 1856, the Prince of Wales, passing under the name of Lord Cavendish and accompanied by two gentlemen, came to Sidmouth and stayed at the Royal York Hotel. He wished to see where his grandfather had died. He visited Woolbrook Cottage, explained who he was, and was shown around the house.

The Royal Glen Hotel
before Glen Road was built.

The Royal Glen's gardens.

The western end of Sidmouth has a great many well-preserved houses, built around 1824, which overlook the shore. **Clifton Cottage** is an old thatched bungalow and next to this are **Beacon** and **Rock Cottage**, two detached houses which face the eastern bay. They appear above **Clifton Place**, a row of terraced houses which was originally known as **Heiffer's Row**, after the fisherman who built them. Clifton Terrace is made up mostly of lodging houses with the exception of Rock Cottage. This belonged to Anna Sutton's great uncle, Thomas Crawley, who in the 1870s used it as a summer residence.

No. 5 Clifton Place was occupied by Lord Le Despencer when he was building Marine Villa (Knowle) about 1810.

No. 1 Clifton Place was a small circular house. At a later date, a square house was built in its place. P. O. Hutchinson watched the building work and described it in his diaries.

Heiffer's Row with houses beyond, showing the small circular house. There are also some small cottages on the beach, these were washed away in heavy storms.

67

In 1847 and 1852 it was resolved by the Sid Vale Association to make good the pathway from the **lime kiln** to the western beach. The lime kiln was situated in what is now **Connaught Gardens.** In 1850 the SVA asked permission of the owner of Peak House and its environs, Mr Lousada, to cut steps down the side of the cliff by the lime kiln to the beach. This developed into a cart track which was used until 1855 to carry limestone to the lime kiln at the top. The path and much of the kiln fell down in about 1870. The public had got so used to having access to the western beach that an extremely long ladder was erected, like Jacob's ladder to heaven, in place of the path. However, the Victorians did not like using the ladder – the clothes they wore were not suitable for climbing, particularly when it was windy, so a new ladder was built.

A P. O. Hutchinson sketch of the lime kiln and the path up from the beach, 3 June 1851.

The apron at the foot of the new 'Jacob's Ladder' completed. However, the esplanade walk around the base of the cliff towards Clifton beach was not completed until the late 1950s.

The ladder replacing the path, 3 June 1871.

The reservoir under construction.

Peak Hill Water Works, 1888. In April 1888 a reservoir was opened on Peak Hill. It was supplied by the Sidmouth Water Co. who collected water from the adjoining hills. The reservoir and filtering beds stood at a considerable height above the town, and this enabled the water to flow to even the most elevated building in the town without assistance from the usual pumping station and its costly machinery.

The sanitary arrangements of the town were good. The system of drainage by sewers was constructed by the Local Government Board and the sewage was conveyed to the sea considerably beyond low-water mark. The sanitary arrangements of hotels and many private houses also underwent considerable improvement. Not only had the most modern water closets been fitted but a system of disconnecting the house drains from the sewers became universal. A system of automatic flushing of the sewers was also in force which gave valuable aid in cleansing and purifying them. The tanks for effecting this operation held 5000–6000 gallons of water and were discharged at periodic times during the day, running through the whole of the sewers.

The reservoir opened in April 1888.

THE TOWN CENTRE

Although deeds from the **parish church** *(Church Street)* have been found indicating the presence of vicars in 1157, 1200 and 1226, it is not until 1259 that a dedication is recorded of a church at Sidmouth – St Giles with St Nicholas. Fragments dating from Norman times, found later, prove that the church must have been of Early English or Decorated style. In about 1450 the church was rebuilt in the Perpendicular style and the tower still remains to corroborate this assertion. In 1789, 1797, 1812 and 1822 work took place to add the north and south aisles, galleries and vestry room against the north wall. There also existed a gallery at the western end of the church in which the organ was placed.

In the rebuilding programme which began in 1860, work consisted of taking down the present chancel and replacing it with two chancel aisles. This involved throwing out a north and south transept and adding one bay to the nave and aisles of the existing church.

Also the roof of the nave was removed and the side walls built up to create a clerestory. The east stained-glass window in the new chancel was installed at this time. The parish was indebted to the generosity of the Rt Hon. and Rev. the Earl of Buckinghamshire for this part of the work. Then the galleries and old seating were removed and new seating installed. After much argument the Earl offered to pay for the removal of the gallery at the west end of the church and the resiting of the organ to allow for the installation of the new stained-glass window presented by Queen Victoria in memory of her father the Duke of Kent who died in Sidmouth in January 1820.

In 1873 Peter Orlando Hutchinson designed and installed four new pinnacles which lasted 100 years. They were given by four residents, the Earl of Buckinghamshire, the Rev. Clements (the vicar), Doctor Radford and Mr Thornton of Knowle.

The tower of the parish church before the pinnacles were added.

The parish church with the pinnacles which were added in 1873.

The Retreat *(Church Street)* is a cottage which was occupied
by curates of the parish church from 1854 to 1855. It is now
the Servicemen's Club, which was established as a memorial
of the 1914–18 war.

71

Hope Cottage *(Church Street)* was built in 1830 and opened as a solicitors' office. The firm began as Messrs Dark & Leicester, then Leicester & Williams, followed by Williams & Radford, Radford & Orchard, Orchard & Michelmore and then Michelmore, Davies & Bellamy. The local magistrates attended to judicial business of an urgent nature at these offices. In 1863 the London & South Western Bank was situated there until it moved to Temple House in 1876. Hope Cottage also housed the Customs and Excise for a time.

Mr G. J. Radford, the solicitor, lived at Sidmount, which was built in 1825, with his two daughters. Sidmouth is much indebted to him for his gift of The Ham (mentioned earlier), and to Miss Radford for the gift of Hope Cottage to the town in 1925.

From 1928 to 1936 it was the offices of the local council. Then it became the town library until 1970. From that time it has been the home of the Sidmouth Museum.

Below: Hope Cottage.

Fort House *(Coburg Road)* was built by Mr Phillips in 1812. It later passed into the hands of Sir John Kennaway, Sidmouth's first MP. It has also been occupied by Mr A. Dashwood and by Sir Francis Bundett.

It was bought by Mr R. A. Wood in 1905 and was converted into two residences and eventually left in trust on condition that it was renamed Church House, although it has no connection with the church.

Coburg Cottage in Coburg Terrace was built in 1830 by Sir John Kennaway for his groom. It was originally known as Windsor Cottage.

The west elevation
of Fort House.

Right:
Coburg Terrace was built in 1815 in Strawberry Hill Gothic
style by Mr John Amyatt, for his cousin Sir John Kennaway.

Below:
Amyatt's Terrace is a row of small terraced houses built by
John Amyatt for his cousin Sir John Kennaway to hide the
view of the churchyard from Fort House and Coburg Terrace
which depressed Sir John.

73

The Old Chancel was the home of Peter Orlando Hutchinson. Although he was on the committee for the restoration of the parish church in 1859, Hutchinson was appalled at the severity of the restoration which left only the tower and the nave arches. He bought the ground adjoining his house, No. 4 Coburg Terrace, and then purchased and re-erected the fifteenth-century chancel from the church, with its fine window, in his new garden. He paid the sum of £45 for it. This eventually became the drawing room of this fascinating house which he built over the next 30 years from 1859.

Above: The chancel rebuilt in P. O. Hutchinson's garden.

Right: The entrance and main house of the Old Chancel.

Below: The chancel after the house had been added.

74

In 1806 it is said that the Fifth Duke of St Albans, a descendant of Charles II and Nell Gwyn, built **Violet Bank Cottage** in Seafield Road and used it to live in during his shore leave. A second floor and balconies have since been added, and it is now Little Court Hotel.

Violet Bank Cottage, built in 1806.

The cottage in 1830 after the addition of the second floor.

Cedar Shade *(All Saints Road)* was originally known as Belle Vue and was built in the early 1800s, when it had a thatched roof. From 1833 to 1835 it was occupied by Mr Edward Barrett and his large family. Whilst living here, Elizabeth Barrett fell under the spell of the Rev. George Hunter, minister of the Marsh Independent Chapel which stood on The Ham. The minister also preached in neighbouring places of worship and a group of Marsh Chapel women would go with him –

Elizabeth was often one of them. Whether she was in love with him we do not know, but he was certainly in love with her. In 1844 he followed her to London, but Robert Browning appeared on the scene and the minister faded into the background. Yet he must have been a clever man to have interested Elizabeth Barrett who was considered for the post of Poet Laureate after the death of Wordsworth in 1850.

Cedar Shade.

The Unitarian Chapel *(All Saints Road)*. During the reign of Charles II there was a congregation of Presbyterians in Sidmouth and it appears that they met in an old barn behind the White Hart Inn. Later, in 1710, a chapel was built on the site of the old barn behind the inn.

Towards the end of the eighteenth century the Presbyterian Church split into two and one branch became the Unitarians. In June 1811 a new chapel was opened and included a Sunday school. Soon after 1811, the Rev. Edmund Butcher became minister and wrote *Sidmouth Scenery & Views, 1818*. The book gives a good description of the town, of many houses, hotels and other establishments. A copy is kept in the Sidmouth Museum Library. In 1884 the adjoining White Hart Inn was demolished and the chapel reconstructed.

The White Hart Inn with the chapel windows at the left-hand end.

Looking down All Saints Road. The White Hart is on the right.

The Unitarian Chapel.

May Cottage *(Blackmore View)* was built in the 1600s, restored in 1830 and owned later by Miss Annie Leigh Browne who let it at a 'peppercorn' rent in 1885. It became Sidmouth's first hospital, with three to four beds in 1889. Soon after 1889, donations were received and Colonel Balfour, the Lord of the Manor, gave some land and a new hospital was built and opened for ten patients. Queen Victoria allowed her name to be given to the hospital – hence the name Victoria Hospital. It was extended in 1916 to fourteen beds and again in 1931 to twenty-seven beds.

Right: May Cottage in about 1820.

Entrance to Victoria Hospital.

Side view
of Victoria Hospital.

High Street

Myrtle Cottage was built about 1800, but demolished in 1888. The Masonic Hall and Myrtle Terrace were built about 1890, and the shopfronts added in the 1950s.

Myrtle Cottage.

Myrtle Cottage being demolished in 1888.

Laying the foundation stone of the new Masonic Hall in 1890.

The Masonic Hall and Myrtle Terrace, before the shopfronts were added.

Many changes have taken place at the southern end of the High Street over the years, as shown in the following photographs. It is interesting to note that at a meeting in July 1891 Sidmouth tradesmen decided to close their shops at 5 p.m. on Thursdays instead of 8 p.m. In those days all shops were kept open until 8 p.m. on weekdays and 10 p.m. on Saturdays.

Left: These cottages in the High Street were demolished in the late 1800s and replaced by Rahere House.

On the left of this photograph the ladies are standing outside the lovely Regency house which was once the home of Dr Bird and then Dr Grant Wilson. Regrettably the house was pulled down and now Woolworth's stands in its place. Mr Fish, the photographer, lived next door in the house on the right. On the corner of Fore Street was T. B. Veale's family grocer and on the right-hand side of High Street is Rahere House which was once the home of Bingley Gibbs Pullen. It later became the National Provincial Bank until 1976, and then S.E.S. Stationers.

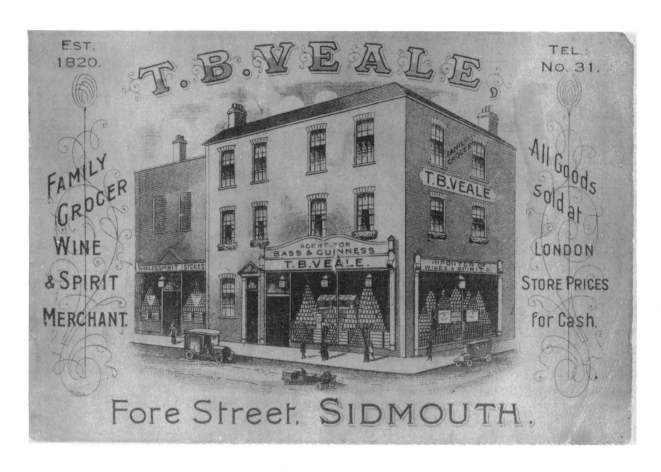

Card advertising T. B. Veale.

Earlier the site had been occupied by Coulson Bros. This photograph gives an interesting view of the street.

Gentleman standing outside what is now Winchesters. On the opposite corner the shop with the thatched roof was Russell's, bakers and confectioners. The side street became known as Russell Street. Mr Russell replaced the shop with a new building.

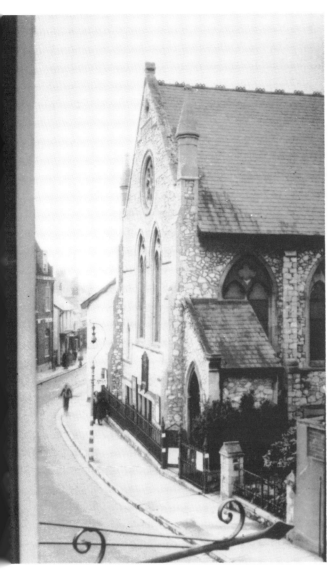

The Methodist Chapel. In 1837 a chapel was built in Mill Street at a cost of £600. It remained in existence until 1882. In that year a Mr Pretty of Ipswich attended the chapel while in Sidmouth for his health, and was not at all enamoured with it. The following year he bought five thatched cottages in High Street for £370 and gave the site to the Wesleyan Society. A new chapel was built on the site and opened in 1885. It cost £1851.19s.8d. to build. Mr Pretty gave £100 to the YMCA to assist them to buy the Mill Street chapel. It is still used by the YMCA today.

A new hall and extension to the chapel was completed in 1964. Then in 1987 the end wall facing High Street was rebuilt.

Above:
The chapel as built in 1885. This photograph was taken in 1931 by Mr Ellis from the window of his photographer's studio at the junction of Holmdale and High Street.

Right:
Interior of chapel taken in 1931 when electricity was installed. The pews on the right under the choir balcony were 'free pews'. Rents were payable for all other pews.

The **Old Ship Inn** stands in Old Fore Street and is in a wonderful state of preservation. It was built in 1350 – a substantial building with cob walls nearly 3 feet thick – and thought to be a monastery long ago. It became an inn and as Sidmouth was one of the chief centres for smuggling in east Devon, the premises were a rendezvous for smugglers. A passage at the back led into Church Lane, which in turn leads to the parish church. From this close connection with the church, magistrates and others of high rank received their share of the contraband. It is well known that a 'sleeping partnership' existed with the smugglers because of the heavy duty payable on brandy and tobacco.

Extensive stables stood at the side and rear of the inn and farmers riding into Sidmouth market used the inn as a meeting place years ago.

The Old Ship Inn in early days.

The Market Place

In 1200 it is recorded that there were sheds, stalls or shops here. The first Market House was a low structure with a painted weathercock. Another Market House was built in 1839 and was purchased from the Manor by Sidmouth Urban District Council in 1903. This building was demolished in 1929 and the present one was built.

In 1883 a conservatory was built at the corner of Old Fore Street and New Street. It had an octagonal dome at one end, a corner of it can be seen in the photograph opposite. Built of glass and iron, it was fitted out for the display of shrubs, plants, fruit, etc. This was a great improvement as it replaced a rubbish yard enclosed by a dirty brick wall.

Later, in 1888, Mr James Pepperell purchased the building and revolutionized the Market Place by erecting a fine building known as Belle Vue Dairy. Mr Maeer built the premises which were later Drewe & Sons.

Right: The Market House as it was built in 1839.

Below:
On the right of the photograph, just beyond the wall of Market House, can be seen the octagonal dome (now Madame Leavesley). On the left is Mortimore the poulterer, which is now Gliddon's.

Looking up Old Fore Street. Mr Pepperell's dairy has
replaced the dome.

Next to Pepperell's on the right was A. C. Drewe the
butcher.

Before **Marlborough Place** was built the site was occupied by St Peter's Chapel. Peter Orlando Hutchinson states that the earliest mention of the chapel was 1322. In later years it was said to have been a school. At one time, the Feoffees of the Poor held their meetings there until the floor became too rotten to support them. The chapel was pulled down in 1805 and Marlborough Place built on the site in 1806.

Looking down Prospect Place to Market House. The premises on the right are now a newsagents, a sports shop and a post office. On the left is Marlborough Place which is now a hotel.

Church Street

The view up Church Street from Market Place in 1849.

Later on the picturesque thatched buildings had deteriorated to a dilapidated condition, and in 1887 they were bought for demolition by the Local Board. A journal of 1888 states that the walls were over 4 feet thick and needed strong efforts by men and horses for their destruction. In an old chimney in the centre of the block were found large slabs of dun-coloured stone. This, along with other indications, showed that the buildings had been constructed between 1574 and 1587. In 1888 a new solid brick building was erected on the site by Mr Gliddon.

Looking down Church Street towards Market Place. On the
right at the corner of Chapel Street is a shop which sold silver
jugs and teapots. It was later a dairy.

On the left of Church Street were old shops which were
smartened up to attract the grand people who came to buy
lace.

Above and right:

In 1927 these cottages and shops were destroyed by fire. Nearly thirty people were rendered homeless and five valuable business premises were gutted. The houses involved were erected some time before 1624. They included Ye Olde Thatched House, The Old Curiosity Shop, The Honiton Lace Emporium and The Dormy House. The right-hand end cottage was renovated, but with a slate roof, and became Willow Cafe. The remainder were rebuilt as shops with flats over.

Ebdons Court off Church Street in the early days. Although the turning still exists the cottages have been rebuilt.

Chapel Street was originally known as Silva Street. It contains **Tudor Cottage** which was built about 1500. Opinion is that Tudor and Merton Cottages were at one time a single Devon longhouse, with roof crucks. The construction is vastly superior to the small dwellings of the fishermen, which indicates that it belonged to an important resident.

During 1972 when work started on modernizing the cottage, an ornamental screen was found and Miss Khristine Ungar successfully restored the panels. One face bears the royal arms of a Tudor sovereign, the other face bears two winged and mermaid-tailed figures facing each other, with two fabulous birds to the south and a cornucopia to the north. It is believed that the screen is as old as the house and that it was decorated either in the reign of Edward VI or early in that of Elizabeth I. Probably there were outbuildings for a stable and open land down to the sea shore. After 1800, with the rapid development of Sidmouth, the views of the sea were blocked. For a detailed description of the house see an excellent article in the Sidmouth Museum, together with photographs of the screen.

Left: Tudor Cottage.

One side of the screen.

Fore Street

The London Hotel has been used for many purposes over the years. On 3 February 1812 a meeting was held to discuss the proposed harbour.

In 1817 the Rev. Butcher tells us that the assembly room here was large and well fitted, and rooms were open for cards every night. During the season there was a ball every Wednesday and large parties were frequently held here. Music was very popular: during the winter a number of both public and private concerts were held. A very respectable band in its infancy, established by some tradesmen in the town, used to amuse the company with martial and other pieces.

In his diary for 1859 P. O. Hutchinson mentions that the Second Devon Artillery Volunteers, then recently formed, mustered at the London Hotel. Later he attended Miss Radford's Ball at the London Hotel, where there were some 150 guests.

On the Prince of Wales' birthday in 1860 the Volunteers fired a twenty-one-gun salute and then retired to the London Hotel where 100 men all dined together.

John Lake and Son were the owners of the London Inn/Hotel and of the livery establishment opposite. For many years coaches and buses had their starting place there, amongst them the famous coaches 'Defiance' and 'Telegraph'. It must have been exhilarating in those far-off days to hear the horns sounding as the coach and four emerged from the stables opposite the hotel.

Above:

In 1913 Sidmouth got its first proper up-to-date picture house, when Mr Ellis converted the Belle Vue Restaurant in Fore Street. Before this the cinematograph was introduced in 1911, when moving pictures were shown at the Manor Hall (now the Manor Pavilion). In those days the films were projected on to the screen from the middle of the hall by the use of limelight. After that the Drill Hall was used for a season, in 1912, when electric lighting was installed and safety appliances were provided.

In 1929 the Grand Cinema was opened but was burnt down in the 1950s. The Radway, which had been built as a theatre, continued as a cinema. The former cinema in Fore Street remained empty for some years until in 1937 it was taken over by Mr Knight and opened as a shop selling ladies' fashions and household linen; it still flourishes today.

Higher up Fore Street was Lakes the omnibus offices (later Notions), shown in this photograph of 1905. The shop next door still sells sweets and tobacco.

93

Cash Dispensing Chemists (later Hinton Lake & Son Ltd, Chemists), built in 1898. A decorative plaster plaque has the initials ERFC, probably those of the owner of Coleberd & Co. Ltd which occupied the building.

Above:
Bovett, a shoe shop (now Boots).

Left:
The business of Trumps was established by Miss Sarah Gove in 1813 and later taken on by her husband, Mr John Trump. Later Mr William Trump, a fine genial man with side whiskers, used to appear in his doorway with a gold watch chain stretched across his imposing figure.

In 1901 Trumps advertised:
Picnic hams @ 5d. per lb
Prime cuts of bacon @ 8d. per lb; Streaky @ 5d. per lb
Cream cheese 6d. each
Old Scotch whisky @ 2/8d. per bottle
Rum @ 2/6d. per bottle
Port @ 1/6d. per bottle
Claret @ 1/– per bottle
Sherry @ 1/10d. per bottle
Champagne @ 4/6d., 5/– and 7/– per bottle

THE SUBURBS

The Hermitage was part of Balsters in Vicarage Road, a farm dating back to 1698 and belonging to Abraham Balster of Membury. Balsters was the farmhouse, the Hermitage was the dairy and the Shrubbery was originally the cowsheds and outhouses. Some of the labourers' cottages were in Elysian Fields. The fields of the farm extended as far as the later Winslade Road. All the roofs were thatched and in the farmhouse the cupboards had solid oak shelves 3–4 in. thick.

The Hermitage in 1826.

Woolcombe House (*Woolcombe Lane*) is of unknown origin: the original deeds appear to have been destroyed and the earliest deeds now in existence are dated 1698.

In about 1834 the house passed into the hands of the Holmes family, builders to the manor, who held it until it was bought by Miss Annie Leigh Browne, early in 1900. The ground floor was used for a children's clinic and the first floor for the activities of the Sid Vale Association. Later, in 1950, it became the Museum. It is now the offices of the Town Council.

Woolcombe House.

The main room on the first floor, with its magnificent roof.

All Saints' Church was built in 1837. Originally called All Saints' Chapel, it was intended as an overflow for the parish church. The Earl of Buckinghamshire and Sir John Kennaway, MP purchased the land and a large house for the parsonage. Stone to build the church came from the quarry at Beer and was given by the Manor Trustees. The cost of building was £3000. In 1871 the church was restored and the vestry was added. All Saints' School next door was built in 1848 for £700 and given by Sir John Kennaway. It was enlarged in 1864.

Below: All Saints' Church.

All Saints' School, 1848.

Above: Manston Old House from a drawing dated 1815.

Manston Old House (*Manstone Lane*) is a two-storey medieval house with walls of rubble and mixed local stone, with a slate roof. The house dates back to 1589, as the moulded chimneypiece, a fine feature, seems to indicate. The date and the initials HM are inscribed on the chimney. The initials are probably those of Henry Morgan of Manston, gent., who married Elizabeth, daughter of Richard, Duke of Otterton. She was the executrix of his will, proved 17 December 1616.

The most important surviving internal feature is the solar on the first floor at the south-east end of the house. This has three arched-brace-collar trusses supporting the roof with wind-braces between purlins. The trusses are joint cruck construction which spring from the ground floor.

The roof feature.

The present front entrance and the chimney with the initials.

99

The Bowd Inn, at the junction of the A3052 and the B3176, was built in 1657. In the late nineteenth century it was occupied by the Batten family. In 1938 Mr Sellick bought the inn. By then it was in a primitive state and he made a number of improvements including the construction of two car parks. The site of the upper car park was formerly an orchard.

The Batten family outside the inn in the late nineteenth century. To the left are members of the Ebden family who lived in the cottage next to the inn.

Sidmouth station (*at the junction of Station Road and Alexandria Road*).

The **railway line** was extended to Sidmouth in 1874. At the official opening on 6 July many residents boarded the first train, the 6.50 a.m. to Sidmouth Junction, and returned in time for breakfast. Later the school children assembled and walked in procession to the station to see the 2.45 p.m. train depart. Great was their wonder if not alarm when they saw and heard the engine for the first time in their lives as it hissed and puffed along the track.

On the Thursday a celebration dinner was given in the grounds of Knowle to upwards of 400 aged and poor people. More than a hundred of them were taken to the station for the journey to the junction and back. They then had tea and when they left they were given silver coins (sixpence, a shilling or a half-crown, according to age) which, it is said, came direct from the Mint.

Station staff in about 1920.
Standing, left to right: –, –, J. Pritchard (W.H. Smith Manager), –, Miss Chown (Booking Clerk), Guard Phillips, Olive Perry (Goods Booking Clerk), Tommy Edwards (Porter), Jimmy Yeo (Signalman), Bill White; *sitting:* Station Master Puggy Faulkner; *on the ground:* Jack Foyle (Guard), Bill White (Junior).

A train at the station in about 1920.

SOME PEOPLE OF SIDMOUTH

Colonel John Edward Hugh Balfour (1863–1952) was the last Lord of the Manor. His father, Mr G. E. Balfour, and his mother both died in 1869, leaving a girl and two boys. Under the terms of his father's will six trustees were nominated upon trust to convey the estate to the testator's eldest son, John, when he reached the age of twenty-five. A house called Broadway, which had previously belonged to General Slessor, was bought in 1872 and pulled down and a new mansion was built on the same site in 1874.

Colonel Balfour was the only Lord of the Manor to reside permanently in Sidmouth. He gave land to the town – 'The Hospital' plot, the three-cornered plot (The Triangle) and The Glen Walk. He was President of the Sid Vale Association until his death in 1952. On his death the Manor was sold – the house to Sidmouth Urban District Council who subsequently resold it as a school, and the farms to their tenants.

Colonel Balfour.

The Manor House (*Broadway*).

Peter Orlando Hutchinson (1810–97) is known for his work in recording Sidmouth's history. He produced a manuscript in five volumes, as well as copious diaries. His poor health as a child meant that he was educated privately, and although he studied architecture briefly he had no profession. But he had plenty of leisure time and the ability to use it well and he developed many interests. He learned to play the piano, the flute and the French horn. He delighted also in sketching, painting, needlework, house repairs, carpentry, gardening and became a geologist, diarist, artist, wood-carver, book-binder and model-maker. He called himself a jack of all trades.

The photograph shows him in his uniform as an officer in the Devon Artillery Volunteers. He was a frequent guest at local houses. Though he did not marry, he admired a pretty face and mentions flirtation, hinting at its dangers. He found he could please the ladies with kisses, sugar plums and Valentine cards. He was happy with his faithful housekeeper, Ann Newton, who served him for 28 years and was left an annuity of £28 for life. (See also p. 74.)

Annie Leigh Browne (1851–1936) and her sister, Lady Lockyer, were the granddaughters of Captain John Carslake, RN, of Cotmaton Hall, who as a midshipman was a member of the crew of HMS *Victory* at the Battle of Trafalgar in 1805. She was a very active member of the Sid Vale Association from 1907 until her death in 1936.

At the turn of the century The Byes was in a poor state; no one wished to accept responsibility for it. So Miss Leigh Browne purchased land on either side of the River Sid between Lovers Walk (opposite Lawn Vista) and Sid Bridge at the bottom of Sid Lane. When she died she left the land to the National Trust. She bought Woolcombe House early in the century (see p. 97) and May Cottage (see p. 78). When she died she left money so that the hall adjoining the Unitarian Chapel could be built in 1938 (see p. 76).

Sir Norman Lockyer.

In 1909, having retired from the position of Director of the Solar Physics Observatory at South Kensington, **Sir Norman Lockyer** built a house on Salcombe Hill (now Brownlands). A plot of ground on the top of Salcombe Hill seemed to be an excellent site for an observatory as it commanded an unbroken view of the horizon and was free from smoke. So with the help of some friends, he started work on this unique enterprise in 1912. Sir Norman became the first director and when he died in 1920 he was succeeded by his son, Dr William J. S. Lockyer, who held the post until his death in 1936. Through the generosity of several donors, including Lady Lockyer, who left the whole of her residuary estate to the Norman Lockyer Observatory Corporation, the observatory was gradually developed. In 1922 a marble memorial plaque was unveiled in memory of Sir Norman and in 1938 a memorial was set up to his son.

After many years of neglect the observatory has been purchased and refurbished by East Devon District Council with the help of The National Trust. It was reopened in October 1989 by Patrick Moore, the well-known astronomer. The Sid Vale Association played a large part in the early negotiations for its restoration.

One of the astronomical domes on Salcombe Hill.

This view of Sir Norman's house with his first observatory shows how ancient man could have timed all the seasons of husbandry. The vertical arrows indicate the azimuth of local sunset throughout the year.

The Earl of Buckinghamshire built Richmond Lodge (now Sidholme) in Elysian Fields in 1826. (See p. 28.) The house was extended as more land was purchased. The music room was added in 1848 and Cumberland Cottage (now the kitchen and ten bedrooms) was added in about 1852.

The Earl financed much of the rebuilding of the parish church and, together with Sir John Kennaway, purchased the ground for All Saints' Church. He also financially supported the local detachment of the 2nd Devon Artillery Volunteers, as recorded in P. O. Hutchinson's diaries.

The Earl had six children by his first wife, Mary, who died in January 1825. In 1826 he married again and had seven children by his second wife, Maria.

Doctor T.H.S. Pullin lived in a house in the High Street, now the offices of Bristol & West Building Society. As a boy he had been educated at the famous Christ's Hospital School where he was esteemed for his fine voice. When the national anthem was sung for the first time, outside St Paul's Cathedral, on Queen Victoria's accession Pullin had the honour of singing it. For 56 years he was in practice in Sidmouth and for nearly 40 years was the town's medical officer of health.

Left: Dr Pullin's house (*High Street*).

Dr Pullin liked hoisting the flag on top of the church tower, as P. O. Hutchinson had done in his time at his own house, The Old Chancel. Here he is hoisting the flag to commemorate the end of the Boer War in 1902. With him are the bellringers. Second left at the back is Jesse Farrant, saddler in Fore Street, next to Boyce the optician. Farrant's youngest son, Norman, was a fruiterer at the top of Lymebourne Avenue. His other sons are in the foreground – Charlie, left, and Sidney, right, who was killed in the First World War.

GOVERNMENT, INDUSTRY AND RECREATION

On 20 May 1863 a **Local Government Board** was formed. It consisted of nine members, all from Sidmouth. The Board's first task was to devise a seal so that official documents could be stamped. There appeared to be nothing already in existence, so a number of ideas were considered and it was decided to adopt P. O. Hutchinson's design of a lug-sail fishing boat on the water. In 1894 the Board was replaced by the Urban District Council.

Below:
Before the Local Board a Manor Court existed. Members of the Court in 1860 are seen here outside the Royal York Hotel. They are: W. Bray, T. Lawrence, Thomas Clark, John Gigg, Mr Lawrence, S. Warren, J. Dimond, R. Gigg, A. Shortland, J. Gigg, J. Chamberland, F. Hook.

The Manor Court Leet. *Sitting, left to right:* Albert Maer, 'Jimmy' Russell, Henry Bastin, W. H. Hasting, James Pepperell and Bobby Gigg; *standing, left to right:* Theo Mortimore, Chippy Charles, John Russell, Alfred Maeer, F. H. Sisterson (biggest), Gigg (smallest), Percy Baron, William Cook, Robert Coles, Abraham Lake, William Battey, and Sam Rowland.

The Town Criers of Sidmouth. The first recorded Town Crier is Thomas Paul. A journal of 1886 stated that he was appointed because he had a 'good sound voice and was able to read well'. Moreover, having been a postman he was acquainted with town matters and as he resided at Prospect Cottage he could easily be found.

Next there was Mr Newton, who was not a native of Devon. He was followed by Theo Mortimore, a Devonian born in Sidmouth, who had a fine burly figure, dark eyes, hair and side whiskers. His strong voice rang out 'Oyez, Oyez', and when in later years he

was presented with a uniform of gold-braided hat, scarlet coat and velvet knee breeches, white stockings and buckle shoes, he caused much interest to visitors. He can be seen in the picture of the Court Leet on page 110. In 1924 he was succeeded by his son Charles Theophilus Carslake Mortimore who was Sidmouth's last Town Crier and who died in 1943.

Theo Mortimore on his three-wheeler bicycle.

Charles Mortimore, Sidmouth's last Town Crier.

The *Remington* arrives in Sidmouth for the launch in 1869.

The Lifeboat. It was not until March 1869 that Sidmouth had its own lifeboat. It was donated by Mrs Remington of Streatham and named *Remington*. Its arrival in Sidmouth was a grand occasion with a procession through the town attended by military bands and the Sidmouth Town Band. The boat was housed in the lifeboat house on the eastern end of the Esplanade. It took part in two sea rescues in 1872, one in 1878 and one in 1883. In 1881 the *Remington* also performed the only recorded rescue of members of the royal family. On 23 May the Duke and Duchess of Edinburgh arrived at Sidmouth on board HMS *Lively* to inspect the lifeboat station. A steam boat was lowered from the ship to take them to the beach, but the swell was rapidly increasing and the craft nearly turned over. Quickly the *Remington* was launched and took on board the Duke and Duchess. After inspecting the coastguard station and the lifeboat (at close quarters!) the Duke and Duchess were driven away in a wagonette with four horses and two postillions over Peak Hill to Otterton and on to Torquay.

Launching the *Remington*.

In 1885 Sidmouth received a larger and more up-to-date lifeboat, the 34-foot *William and Francis*, equipped with water ballast for stability. The new boat was also designed to be self-righting. She had to wait until 1911 for her one and only rescue and the station was closed down in 1912. In total Sidmouth's lifeboats had saved thirty-four lives.

111

Above:
Hauling the *William and Francis* from the boathouse and down the beach.

The crew and coastguards with the *William and Francis*.

The Fishermen of Sidmouth. Fishing was the mainstay of life in Sidmouth during the eighteenth and nineteenth centuries. Early in 1900 there were some twenty-three drifters operating from the beach, which extended from the lifeboat house at the eastern end to Fort Cottage in the west. A very interesting small book by Vernon Bartlett, which gives details of all the families involved with Sidmouth fishing, is obtainable in the Museum. Every family of fishermen had their section of the beach and this ancient 'right' was honoured by everyone. About 1909 the fishing was already failing locally and the sudden disappearance of the herring, the main source of income in winter, brought about the 'big exodus' when fishermen were forced to find jobs ashore, some locally and some as far afield as Australia, Canada and South Africa.

Some of the fishermen of 1888 with the drifter *Storm Petrel*. *Back row, left to right:* Turk Cordey, Ruder Pike, Sam Ware, Fred Bartlett, Punch Woolley, Fred Ware, Bill Ware; *front row, left to right:* Banty Hook, Jim Bartlett, Jack Tapley, George Horn, Charles Soloman, Dick Soloman.

The fishermen's cricket team outside the Pavilion on Fortfield, 1884. *Back row:* J. Farrant, Turk Cordey, F. Ware, F. Bartlett, C. Soloman, Jim Bartlett; *front row:* H. Newton, Smallridge, C. Pursey, J. Conant, G. Horn, D. Soloman.

113

Sam Ware.

B. Ware, Dan Hooke, Fred Farrant, Townsend
and Chips the dog.

Sam Woolley.

Tom Woolley.

The lace industry began in the seventeenth century and reached its peak in the nineteenth century. In east Devon some 3600 were employed in lace making, 300 of whom were in Sidmouth. It was mainly women who were employed in the industry, together with many children who attended lace schools from the age of five and became experts. The work was hard and needed close concentration in good light; this is why the lace makers used to sit outside their cottages in summer and winter.

Lace made locally was taken to lace traders in Sidmouth. These men paid for the lace not with money but with groceries and other goods not always needed by the workers. The traders made large profits. From them the lace went to a centre in Honiton, whence it was sent to London, hence the name 'Honiton lace'. In 1810 lace-making machines were introduced and this led to unemployment for women and children. However, opportunities for domestic work were afforded by the increasing affluent society in Sidmouth.

Behind the cottages at the top of the High Street was Pike's Court where Elizabeth Denner lived after she married Fred Smith. She was frequently to be seen making lace outside her cottage.

Above:
Postman Banks is seen here with his pony and trap outside Sidbury Post Office in 1914. He resigned in 1919 after nearly 35 years of service.

The royal post cart that took the mail from Sidmouth to Exeter, standing at St David's Station, Exeter.

Left:
Postman John ('Jack') Sparks and his wife in their garden. He started his service as a local postman in 1879 working as a 'Sunday sub' to Sidbury at a wage of 1/6d a week. In December of that year he went on the Branscombe round at at salary of 14/- a week. In 1880 he began a morning round embracing the district from Arkell's town brewery to Woolbrook and Core Hill at a wage of 7/- a week. The low rate of pay in those days explains why so many postmen occupied their spare time with bootmaking, tailoring and other jobs.

From 1882 Postman Sparks did the double walking round to Sidbury and later he was transferred to town. He was appointed Head Postman in 1906.

There were two breweries in the town. **Vallance's Brewery** occupied a prominent position in Temple Street and Brewery Lane and dated back to 1832 when it was known as Harvey & Vallance. **Arkell's Brewery** was behind the Old Ship Inn in Old Fore Street and was established some time early in the nineteenth century.

Below: The staff of Vallance's Brewery.

The staff of Arkell's Brewery.

Local bands. It is reported that in about 1818 a very respectable band then in its infancy, established by some tradesmen in the town, in fine weather amused the public with martial airs and other pieces. This early interest was developed and the Sidmouth Excelsior Band, shown here in 1885, became well established.

It is reported in a journal of 1891 that the Volunteer Band performed a selection of music at Coulson's Corner in High Street (now a gift shop at the junction of Fore Street and Old Fore Street). At the same time the Town Band played a selection on the Esplanade opposite the Royal York Hotel. It is said that 'messengers' would be sent from one band to the other to see which had the larger audience.

The Excelsior Band 1885 outside the Old Chancel. *Back row:* G. Farrant, F. W. Macleod, Wallace Dowell; *middle row:* F. Farrant, Frederick Pinney, William Holmes, R. J. Russell, A. Slade, H. Russell (Conductor), J. Russell, G. Berwick, A. Bacon, Adolphus Farrant, N. Skinner, P. Dimond; *front row:* G. Bartlett, J. Ebdon, Jack Russell, G. Turner, Fred Whitton.

There are eight bells in the tower of **St Giles with St Nicholas.** Before the time of Charles I there was only one, though no date is shown on the bell. That is the original pre-Reformation bell, now no. 6. In 1667 one other was added, which is now no. 5; in 1708 the fourth, seventh and eighth were added; in 1844 the present third was put up. In 1869 the bells were rehung as by then the frame was in decay. In 1875 Mr R. N. Thornton of Knowle gave the two smallest bells, completing the octave.

The ringers for the Relief of Mafeking, May 1900. *Back row, left to right:* R. Newberry, 2nd, W. Turner, 7th, A. Pile, tenor, J. Colwill, 5th, J. Farrant, 6th; *front row, left to right:* G. Youldon, 3rd, T. Pinney, 4th, G. Conant, foreman, treble. The tower bells were rung for this occasion.

118

The Fire Brigade. The existence of thatch within the town greatly increased the risk of fire. Once alight thatch went up like a torch. Between 1875 and 1890 there were nineteen serious fires and the fire engine could not cope at all. In 1902 Mr Wood of Belmont gave the town a new fire engine and on 5 June it was put through its paces on The Ham, flashing up its boiler and raising a full head of steam very rapidly.

Above:
The fire engine on The Ham. Mrs Lee of Winslade Road gave this photograph and on the extreme right is her grandfather Mr Piper, father of two well-known gardeners, Harry and Albert. Next to him is Supt. J. Skinner who was called to Mrs Schofield's shop at Radway when it caught fire. He rushed up the stairs and came down backwards followed by the stock of pencils rolling down! After a few tries he sat down and said, 'Let 'er burn up a bit so that we can see were we'm going.' His men were always expecting his breath to catch fire!

Left: At full gallop to a fire.

Transport. William Albert Dagworthy (1873–1951), known as WAD, was an early enthusiast of motor transport. His parents had settled in a little house between the Bedford Hotel and the present Torbay Hotel and several children were born to them there. But WAD's father left the family and went to America and did not return. WAD, as the middle son, was left to look after the family. He courted May Deanbank of Solihull very strenuously, for it took him two days to get there by bicycle!

When he realized the importance of the automobile, he changed from repairing horse-drawn vehicles to cars and the little house quickly became surrounded by his garage. (This area is now occupied by Western Court.)

Sidmouth Cycling Club.
Back row, left to right: Tintack Sellek, –, Alf Taylor, Teddy Mitchell, Chippy Charles, Sergeant Doyle, ?Jim Pepperell, – Vallance, Pemberthy, chemist.

Front row, left to right: W. Prideaux, –, Toot Youlden, Jim Hoskins, ?J. Trick, Harry Russell, ?Jim Russell, Col. Hughes, H. G. Macleod, ?Vallance, Jim Colwill, Bill Dean the baker, ?Jack Snell, Bill Dagworthy, –, Jimmy Clark.

Horse-drawn carriages on the Esplanade.

A party ready for an outing.

A float in the Sidmouth Carnival.

WAD in one of his early cars.

WAD has his first repair depot.

Irving, WAD's son, takes some passengers for a ride. *On the offside, left to right:* Irving Dagworthy, B. Churchill, C. Harris, Bill Gooding, – Broom, Moss Turner; *nearside, left to right:* J. Skinner, R. Harris, Dr Blake the vet, ?B. Slade, R. Simmons, W. Hook, councillor.

Sidmouth Golf Club was formally registered with the Royal and Ancient on 16 October 1889. The links at that time consisted of six holes, played thrice in matches, but soon afterwards they were extended to nine holes. In 1905 an eighteen-hole course was laid out and a new club house built.

When Colonel Balfour, an honorary member, died in 1952 the Balfour Manor, including the golf course, was sold. Sidmouth Urban District Council made a compulsory purchase before the club was offered at public auction.

The first club house being built in 1889.

1905, enlarged in 1920 and extended in 1989.

The **Sidmouth Mummers** regularly performed the mummers play around the town. This picture was taken in 1904 and was presented by the late Councillor Stan Baker, whose father, Arthur, is on the far left. *Back, left to right*: Arthur Baker, Fred Baker, George West, Michael Bovett; *front, left to right*: Fred Tucker, Bart Fox, Robert Leash.

Two pictures of the parade to celebrate **Queen Victoria's Golden Jubilee** in 1887. Troops and local volunteer societies took part.

INDEX